READ AND RETELL

A Strategy
for the
Whole-Language/Natural Learning
Classroom

Hazel Brown and Brian Cambourne

Heinemann
Portsmouth, NH

HEINEMANN
a division of Reed Elsevier Inc.
361 Hanover Street, Portmouth, NH 03801–3912
Offices and agents throughout the world

First published in the United States in 1990 by Heinemann
Reprinted 1990, 1992, 1993, 1994, 1996, 1997
First published in 1987 in Australia
Nelson ITP Australia
102 Dodds Street
South Melbourne 3205

ISBN 0 435 08506 9

Designed by Leanne McConnell
Cover photograph by Howard Birnstihl, Northside Productions
Typeset in Paladium and Helios by Midland Typesetters
Printed in China by L Rex Printing Co

READ AND
RETELL

Contents

1

What It's All About

This book is about a teaching strategy which we began experimenting with several years ago. Originally it was one of several activities which we thought might be useful to teachers who were wanting to implement what has become known as a 'wholistic/natural learning' approach to literacy teaching.

However, as we came to understand the full implications of the model of learning we were trying to work within, we realised that the particular activity which we had labelled the 'retelling procedure' had enormous potential as an all-purpose, extremely powerful learning activity. Not only did it encapsulate all the principles of the wholistic/natural learning model, but it had many characteristics which teachers find attractive and useful:
- easy to prepare
- suitable for a whole range of language abilities
- flexible in its use
- requiring a minimum of teacher involvement
- providing 'on-task' practice of a range of literacy skills (reading, writing, listening, talking, thinking, interacting, comparing, matching, selecting and organising information, remembering, comprehending).

It also provided a direct and sensitive index of growth and development in a wide range of literacy learning. The more we experimented with it, the more we realised just how useful a strategy it could be, and it soon became one of the regular activities in the whole-language/natural learning experiment we were running.

In this book we have tried to systematise what we found out about the retelling procedure, so that teachers who would like to use it in ways that maximise their pupils' literacy learning have a ready-made set of retelling sessions with which to begin.

The Retelling Procedure—What Is It?

Perhaps the best way to answer this question is to engage you in a written retelling. We can simulate a typical retelling session for you and you will, vicariously, get a feel for the potential of the procedure. The rest of the book will then make a lot more sense to you.

A simulated retelling session

Imagine you are in a group of four or five in a classroom and the teacher hands you a sheet of quarto paper which obviously has print on it. You can't read the print because the sheet has been folded and all that is visible is what appears to be the title. This is what you and the other members of your group are handed:

Your teacher then says: 'On this sheet of paper is a fable. We've been reading a lot of fables lately, but I don't think you've read this one before. You listen while I read the title to you.' (She reads the title.) 'I'd like you all to write down a prediction. What might a fable with a title like that be about? Just take a few minutes to write down what you think could happen in a fable with a title like that. Don't worry too much about spelling or neatness. No one else is going to read it.'

If you have access to a pen and paper we'd like you to take a minute or two to attempt something similar. Make a prediction. What might be the story of a fable with that title?

If you were in that imaginary classroom your teacher would then ask you to share your prediction with the others in the group. In fact you would all read your predictions to the rest of the group. Anyone who wanted to could comment. You would probably find that all your fellow students' predictions were sensible and plausible, even though each one was different. You would each probably talk for a few minutes about the predictions you made. Then your teacher would say something like: 'Well, let's open the sheet up now and read it through.'

This is what you would see.

The Scotty Who Knew Too Much

James Thurber

Several summers ago there was a Scotty who went to the country for a visit. He decided that all the farm dogs were cowards, because they were afraid of a certain animal that had a white stripe down its back. 'You are a pussycat and I can lick you,' the Scotty said to the farm dog who lived in the house where the Scotty was visiting. 'I can lick the little animal with the white stripe too. Show him to me.'

'Don't you want to ask any questions about him?' said the farm dog.

'Nah,' said the Scotty. 'You ask the questions.'

So the farm dog took the Scotty into the woods and showed him the white-striped animal and the Scotty closed in on him, growling and slashing. It was all over in a moment and the Scotty lay on his back. When he came to, the farm dog said, 'What happened?'

'He threw vitriol,'* said the Scotty, 'but he never laid a glove on me.'

A few days later the farm dog told the Scotty there was another animal all the farm dogs were afraid of. 'Lead me to him,' said the Scotty. 'I can lick anything that doesn't wear horseshoes.'

'Don't you want to ask any questions about him?' said the farm dog.

'Nah,' said the Scotty.'Just show me where he hangs out.' So the farm dog led him to a place in the woods and pointed out the little animal when he came along. 'A clown,' said the Scotty, 'a pushover,' and he closed in, leading with his left and exhibiting some mighty fancy footwork. In less than a second Scotty was flat on his back, and when he woke up the farm dog was pulling quills out of him.

'What happened?' said the farm dog.

'He pulled a knife on me,' said the Scotty, 'but at least I have learned how you fight out here in the country, and now I am going to beat you up.' So he closed in on the farm dog, holding his nose with one front paw to ward off the vitriol and covering his eyes with the other front paw to keep out the knives. The Scotty couldn't see his opponent and he couldn't smell his opponent and he was so badly beaten that he had to be taken back to the city and put in a nursing home.

Moral: *It is better to ask some of the questions than to know all the answers.*

*vitriol (vit're-ol'): literally, sulfuric acid.

Now compare your prediction with the actual text. How close were you? Were you on course or was your prediction different? Where do you think you got the idea for the prediction which you made? If you were really in a group, what kinds of predictions do you think your fellow group members might have made?

Imagine now that your teacher says something like this: 'Read it through a few times until you're sure you really understand it, then put it to one side and, without referring back to it, pretend that you have to write to someone who hasn't read the story. Retell as much of it as you can, so that they can enjoy it and understand nearly as much as you did. Remember, this is not a test or something you should get anxious about. You shouldn't try to read and memorise special bits or words, because if you do, you won't understand the whole story. Just read it for enjoyment and then retell it. You don't have to use the author's words, and you don't have to remember the whole lot, which would be impossible anyway. You can express the meanings in your own words if you want to. I'm more interested in how you interpret it than in the amount you remember.'

If you would like to continue the exercise yourself, close the book and, without referring back to it, retell the Thurber story yourself.

If you were really in that imaginary classroom, your teacher would ask you to share and compare your retelling with someone else. You would then spend some time reading your own version, the original story and your partner's version and discussing any number of aspects of how they were alike or different.

So that you can get an idea of what that discussion might be like, let us imagine these are the retellings your fellow group members produced.

Compare yours with the three on pages 5 to 8. Which is most like yours? Which is least? How do they differ? How are they alike? Who do you think was the better reader? Why do you think that? Who has most control over the written form of language? Why do you say that? What did you forget to include in your retelling that others remembered? What did you change? What did they change?

If we told you that one of the samples was a retelling done by a doctoral student, and the others were done by a Grade 6 boy and a Grade 2 girl, could you guess which was which? How?

If you had really taken part in a session like this, we would argue that you have used language in some very complex and cognitively demanding ways. If you did it regularly, you would be engaging in a learning activity which provided opportunity for you to gain a high degree of control over some of the ways in which you were using the language.

Long ago there was a scotty who went out to visit the country to see the farm dogs. Who he thought were cowards. When he got there the farm dog was there. The farm dog "In the wood there was a animal with a white stripe down its back." "Lead me to him." "Whie don't you want any quegens" "Noh" "You herd I said" The farm dog led him to the woods. The scotty crawled in a few moments it was over the scotty was lieing on his back. The next day back to the farm dog. The farm dog led me to him "The farm dog said "There is a thing with knives on it's back" led me to him" "Whie dont you want any quegens" "You herd what I said" The farm dog led him to the woods where the thing was. The scotty said "I can fight any thing that doesn't have a horse shoe" They came to the thing the scotty crawled in the moment the scotty was lieing on his back. He said "I know how to fight now." He was so badly hert that he had to get sent to the city nursry

the end

One day a scotty went on a holiday to the country. He thought that all the farm dogs were sissys* because they were afraid of an animal that had a white stripe down its back. 'Show me this animal', the scotty said "I will beat him up".

"Don't you want to ask any questions about this animal?"

'Nah' the scotty said.

The farm dog led him into the forest.

A while later they came to this animal and the scotty approach the animal.

A few moments later it was all over and the scotty lay on his back

"What happened?' the farm dog said.

"He through vitriol* at me and knocked me flat" The scotty said

Later on the farm dog told him about another animal

"Show him to me" the scotty said "I'll turn him into mince meat!"

"Don't you want to ask any questions

?" the farm dog asked.

"Nah" the scotty said

Once again the farmdog took the scotty into the middle of the forest. There they ~~met~~ met a animal. The scotty closed in Growling and showing some mighty good foot work.

Not long after he was lying on his back

when he ~~came~~ came to the farmdog asked "What happened"

"He stuck knives into me" the scotty answered "but now I know how to fight.

The next day ~~he~~ he fought them with his ~~nose~~ nose blocked and his eyes ~~covered~~ covered. He was a complete failure because he couldn't smell his enemy and he couldn't see it. He was so badly hurt that he got sent to a dog home and got a proper nursing.

Moral: Never ask the questions before ~~~~ you know the answers

*Sulfuric acid

A city dog, a scotch terrier went to visit a farm where he was being shown around by a resident farm dog. The scotch terrier was an egotistical mutt who believed himself to be a pretty tough customer. The farm dog, in the course of conversation informed the scotch terrier that there were a couple of tough customers around the district. The egotistical scotch terrier, without waiting to find out any details of these tough customers declared he could lick them. The first of these animals was described as a "pussy" cat with a white stripe. Really it was a skunk, and upon meeting it, the scotch terrier, without finding out any more about the skunk rushed in to fight (using traditional methods). One squirt and it was all over. After the fight ~~it was all over~~ the scotch terrier was filled with excuses. (he threw vitriol over me). The second opponent was a porcupine. The scotch terrier did the same thing and ended with quills in his eye and face.

The story concludes with a moral which relates to the old proverb

. Fools rush in where angels fear to tread".

The Retelling Procedure and Language Use

What is involved in completing such a retelling? Here is a list of the range of different ways in which a participant in a retelling session uses language skills:

1. The retelling procedure (as we define it) involves participants in some intensive reading, writing, talking and listening, around a central theme. In other words, all the traditional language arts are involved in a collaborative way. Reading and talking are mutually supportive, and each is supported by, and supports, writing and listening.

2. The sharing and comparing phases of the procedure demand intense listening and evaluation of others' use of language and interpretation of meaning.

3. Sharing and comparing also coerces multiple readings and re-readings of at least three different texts: the original text, the participant's own retelling of it, and at least one peer's retelling of it. These multiple re-readings are characterised by a high degree of active engagement with the texts.

4. The sharing and comparing phases of the procedure also demand continual shifts of focus, from meaning at the whole story level, to the individual word, to interpetation of phrases, back to the whole story again, as the need arises.

5. Because the participant has made some predictions about the meanings in the story, the first reading of the original text is characterised by a concentration on meaning and the comprehension of meaning. (Was my prediction accurate?) This is what research consistently advocates as the proper focus of any reading act.

6. During the actual written retelling phase, the reteller is engaged in a whole range of significant language processes, including literal recall of events, characters, main points, rhetorical features, stylistic devices and text structure.

7. In addition, the reteller, when writing the retelling, must engage in a continuous cycle of different cognitive activities, including the selection of information and rhetorical and stylistic devices, the organisaton and summarising of information, and paraphrasing.

8. While reading the original text, reading a peer's retelling, and creating (i.e. writing) his or her own retelling text, the participant is continually engaging and re-engaging with spelling and punctuation conventions.

9. In the sharing and comparing phase which follows the actual writing of the retelling, participants give and receive responses that coerce reflection upon, and discussion of, a wide range of text-related concepts. They are learning how to act upon written language as an object external to themselves. They are learning the vocabulary and skills of talking about

written language. This is another way of saying they are learning to operate at a 'meta-linguistic' level.

We discovered that all these activities, if engaged in regularly, combine to bring about some very important and valuable literacy learning. Some of this learning is described in the next section.

The Effects of the Retelling Procedure

As we said earlier, the potential of the retelling procedure as a language-learning activity was not immediately obvious to us. We originally regarded it merely as a useful group or whole-class activity to keep children usefully engaged in a whole-language classroom. As we continued to use it, however, a number of things became obvious to us:

1. There was evidence of a great deal of incidental, almost unconscious, learning of text structures, vocabulary and conventions of written language taking place. While this had been hoped for and expected, we did not expect it to be as pervasive, durable and intense as it turned out to be.

2. There was repeated evidence of what we decided to call 'linguistic spillover' from the retelling sessions. We coined this term to describe the reappearance of certain linguistic forms, structures, concepts and conventions, which had been encountered in the texts used in retelling sessions. Sometimes this spillover occurred weeks or months later. We believe this was clear evidence that internalisation had taken place. This was an important discovery for us for we realised that we could maximise the probability of certain kinds of text features being learned if we chose the retelling pieces appropriately.

3. We noticed an enormous growth in the confidence of our young learners when approaching tasks that involved reading, writing and talking. When we tried to ascertain the source of this confidence, our interviews and other records showed that it was closely associated with their experiences during retelling sessions. They told us such things as:
- 'Retelling sessions help me read better and understand more.'
- 'Retelling lessons help me with spelling and punctuation.'
- 'They (retelling sessions) give me lots of ideas for my own writing, like ways to achieve certain special effects.'
- 'When we share our retellings I learn a lot about how other people read, write and remember, and that helps me later. Like when I've got a similar problem, I think "Now how did Neil solve that?", and I remember and I do it.'
- 'When we share our retellings I learn how to say and use words that I didn't know before, like "the fairy bade her turn around three times". I'd never heard "bade" before and when I read the fable I thought I knew what it meant, but I wasn't too sure. When Todd talked about that word in our sharing, then I really knew what it meant.'

- 'When we predict what the title will be about, and when we try to list words that might be in the story, you know, at the beginning of the retellings, then I know if I know a lot or a little bit about the topic.'
- 'I like retellings, especially when we share, because other kids are always interested in what my retelling will be. I like it when they say things like: "I wished I'd have put that." or "I like the way you've used that word instead of the one in the story". I feel good when they say things like that.'

4. We also noticed growth in what we called '**reading flexibility**'. By this, we mean the ability to change reading 'gears' from almost casual skim-reading to a very intense and deep engagement with the text, or from a global to a molecular level of focus and back again. As time passed, our young learners developed the facility to change reading gears to an unexpected degree.

As part of the experiment we spent some time merely observing the children when engaged in the different kinds of reading that take place in a whole-language classroom. We found that the reading behaviour which typically occurred during the retelling sessions was different in a number of aspects from that observed during sustained silent reading (SSR). For example, there were more readings of the same text. The first reading was usually a quick scan. We discovered that this was because they wanted to check how good their predictions were. Their subsequent readings were similar to those occurring during SSR.

However, during the discussions which occurred after the retelling, the reading behaviour changed significantly again. While sharing their written retellings they searched carefully through different parts of their retelling text, the original text and their partners' texts. They read and re-read and re-read again and generally engaged with texts in ways which were of a quite different intensity from those employed during SSR. The discussions which they had and their overt behaviour showed quite clearly that they shifted their levels of focus from global slabs of meaning, down to the nuances of individual words, down to the features of spelling and/or punctuation, and then back again with ease. In other words, they seemed able to range over the whole spectrum of levels of text, from global meaning to word level meaning, down to micro-conventions like colons, and back again without much difficulty at all.

There was also an increase in what could be called 'supportive reading', i.e. two readers helping each other work through different parts of a text, either by discussing how they'd arrived at their interpretations or by reading along together.

In summary, it would be fair to assert that the retelling procedure as we used it was accompanied by a number of different kinds of growth. We observed growth in:

- knowledge of text forms
- knowledge of text conventions
- the conscious awareness of processes involved in text construction
- the range and variety of text forms and conventions being employed in other writing tasks

- control of vocabulary
- reading flexibility
- confidence.

We believe that growth in these areas is a good thing as far as literacy education is concerned. This is not to imply that these areas of growth represent an exhaustive or finite set of the characteristics of literacy. We are, however, prepared to argue that continued and steady growth in these areas of language behaviour is conducive to the development of sufficient control over the written form of the language to meet the literacy needs that modern society expects from the graduates of its school system.

What Literacy Education Ought To Be About

We said earlier that the retelling procedure was originally devised as a useful activity in something called a 'whole-language/natural learning classroom'. Like all educational enterprises, the whole-language/natural learning view of literacy is guided by a certain philosophy. At the very beginning of this experiment, to devise our aims and objectives, we asked ourselves certain 'philosophical' questions about what we were trying to achieve:

- What are we trying to achieve with respect to reading and writing development with these children?
- With respect to literacy, what kinds of learners do we wish to emerge from this class at the end of the school year?
- What is it we wish the children in this class to be able to do as readers and writers?

These are basic questions about aims and objectives, and how they are answered determines to a large extent how one goes about organising a literacy curriculum. We found that a wholistic approach to literacy education demands a wholistic approach to aims and objectives. Just as one cannot fragment language into what appear to be logical sets of sub-skills and sub-concepts, so one cannot fragment aims and objectives into stages or class levels or sets of specific aims.

Here are the aims we finally decided should guide the literacy program we were testing.

Aim 1: To help our learners become aware of, and understand, the power of reading and writing. In particular, to lead them to a conscious awareness of the potential of reading and writing as a means of developing both thinking and learning, and as a means of modifying, creating and extending learning and thought. (Rationale: Our society values and rewards those who learn and think. Learning and thinking are enhanced through control of language forms. Reading and writing lead to control of language forms, especially if learners are consciously aware of how the two activities support and extend each other.)

Aim 2: To produce learners who are confident about their abilities to use reading and writing for a whole range of thinking and learning tasks.

(Rationale: Learning is enhanced if learners are confident about their ability to learn.)

Aim 3: To produce learners who will continue to read and write long after formal instruction had finished. (Rationale: Once learned, the skills of literacy ought to be durable. The probability of such skills enduring is increased if learners are positive about them. Effective learning is facilitated if the learners have positive attitudes towards what is being learned.)

We believe that the kinds of growth observed during the experiment with the retelling procedure all contributed to the more general aims we were trying to achieve. It is difficult to attribute any one single kind of growth to the achievement of any one or two specific aims. Growth in one area seems both to feed off and to encourage growth in other areas.

For example, we believe that growth in confidence is a function of being consciously aware of the processes which can be used to construct texts, which can, in turn, be affected by and effect growth in the knowledge of text forms. In a similar fashion, confidence is also boosted by the knowledge that one is developing control over the conventions of text which the society values; this, in turn, is aided and abetted by growth in the range and variety of text forms being studied.

Similarly, a conscious awareness of the power of reading and writing as a tool for thinking and learning is a function of the control that one manages to attain over different kinds of textual forms (genre). This is also helped by the ability to read flexibly as the purposes and contexts of reading change.

Finally, learners will continue to use the skills of literacy (i.e. they will be durable), only if they are growing in confidence, and knowledge, and are consciously aware that they are indeed 'growing'. In other words, the kinds of growth which we observed to be taking place — and for which we gave the credit to regular and systematic engagement in the retelling procedure — were fundamental to the achievement of the aims we'd set for the children's literacy development.

An Extra Benefit from Regular Use of the Retelling Procedure

As well as noting these kinds of growth in our pupils, we also found that the retelling procedure helped the teacher with the task of **evaluating and assessing literacy growth**. The written retellings which learners produced (what we called their 'retelling texts'), **and their behaviour while they produced them**, became valuable sources of information about literacy development. We found that if we sampled our learners' written retellings over time, and used them in conjunction with other information, we could make evaluative statements about their:
- reading ability
- control of various genre

- control of many aspects of the writing process
- control of the conventions of written language.

In the following chapters we shall elaborate on how to use the retelling procedure so that its potential can be fully realised. First, however, we need to examine the reasons (i.e. the 'theory') which make it such a powerful learning activity.

2

The Phenomenon of
Linguistic Spillover

When we first began documenting what happened when the retelling procedure became a regular classroom activity, one particular outcome stood out. It was that **many of the features of the text which the children had been asked to read and retell when engaged in a retelling procedure were obviously being internalised by the children.**

This internalisation revealed itself in two ways:

First, we noticed that the children's written retellings contained many of the features of the original text. At first we didn't take much notice of this because it was, after all, the object of the retelling – to reproduce the original from memory. And this is indeed what happened. All the children who engaged in retellings reproduced in various degrees of completeness, the original text. In other words, their written retellings contained some or all of the events, characters, and other aspects of the meanings in the original text. In some instances, some of the same phraseology and vocabulary found its way into the written retellings. While we partly expected this, we also noted that certain textual features such as the use of colons, the separation of speech from other parts of the text, the spellings of words which they had never used before, were also appearing in the written retellings. We called this 'direct spillover'.

An Example of Direct Spillover

The example reproduced below was written after reading the story 'The Old Woman Who Lived in a Vinegar Bottle', printed above it. Note that the speech is separated, a colon is used, language like *bade* appears, words like *mansion* and *draughty* are spelt correctly and *vinegar* is finally spelt correctly.

The Old Woman Who Lived in a Vinegar Bottle

There was once an old woman who lived in a vinegar bottle. One day a kind fairy happened to be passing by and she heard a voice moaning:

'What a shame, what a shame. Why do I have to live in a vinegar bottle when a little cottage with a pretty garden would be so much better?'

The kind fairy took pity on the old lady and told her to close her eyes and turn around three times. This the old lady did and found herself in the loveliest cottage with a small but pretty rose garden surrounding it.

Many months passed and the kind fairy came by the little cottage and heard a grumbling voice saying:

'What a shame, what a shame. Why do I have to live in a **pokey** little cottage when a big **mansion** would be nicer?'

The fairy was surprised to hear these words but again took pity on the old woman, **bade** her close her eyes and turn around three times. When this was done, a mansion with wide sweeping lawns had replaced the cottage. Happy with her good deed, the fairy flew away to look for other people to help. It was many months before she was back that way but, lo and behold, what should she hear but a whining voice saying:

'What a shame, what a shame. Why should I have to suffer a draughty mansion like this when a royal palace and servants would make me far more comfortable? I want to be a queen and rule over the people.'

The fairy was angry to hear this but once again told the old woman to close her eyes and turn around three times. When she had done this the old woman had a crown on her head, wore splendid clothes and had a magnificent palace as her home, from which to rule over all the land and the people.

Many months later the fairy stopped by to visit the old woman but she flew into a rage when she heard the complaining voice again:

'What a shame, what a shame. Why should I have to live in such a small palace and rule over such a small country when I could rule over the whole world?'

So once again the kind fairy bade the woman turn around three times. This the old crone did but when she opened her eyes she found herself back in the vinegar bottle. The kind fairy didn't visit the old lady ever again.

The old woman who lived in a vinigar bottle

24·3·86

I think this story is about a old woman who
is so small that she can fit in a vinager
bottle and she has a lot of kids so
she moves it to an old viniger bottle
she finds at the dump.

There was once a old woman who lived
in a vinigar bottle. One bright day a kind
fairy happened to be passing when the
old woman ~~es~~ grumbled:

"What a shame, what a shame.
why do I have to live in a viniger
bottle when a small cottage would
be much nicer!"

When the fairy heard this she bade
the old woman to turn ~~aron~~ around
three times with her eyes shut tightly.
So the old women did what the fairy
told her.
In a wink of her eye she was in
a small rose garden at the back of
a lovely cottage with a thatched
roof.
A few monthes later the kind fairy
come ~~bace~~ back to visit the old
woman but yet again she heard
a moan:

"What a shame, what a shame
why do I have to live in a pokey
old cottage when I ~~coue~~ could live
in a magnificent mansion."

So ~~once~~ once again the kind
fairy ~~&~~ told the old woman to
close her eyes and turn around
three times.
Again the old woman did as she
~~ha~~ was told and found herself in

what she had wished for, a mansion. But still the old woman was not grate-full she wanted but ~~still~~ but more and more. So when the ~~o~~ kind fairy passed again she heard more whines saying.

"what a shame, what a shame Why do I have to live in a huge and draughty old mansion when I could live in a palace and rule over the country."

So again she told the woman to turn around 3 times with her eyes shut. This time the old woman found herself crowned ~~&~~ queen of her country with servents waiting on her. The next time the fairy past the old women winged:

'What a shame, what a shame why couldn't I rule over the world?'

Then the fairy was well and true ly very, very angry so she told the old woman once more to turn around 3 times with her eyes shut. But this time the old woman did not find her- self where she had wished instead she found herself back in her small, dusty old vinegar bottle.

While we had expected this kind of spillover, we hadn't really expected it to such a degree because we did not think that young children would have such efficient memories. We simply attributed this phenomenon to rote memorisation.

However, when we questioned our subjects about what they'd actually focused on as they were reading (before the act of writing the retelling), they told us our explanation was wrong. They adamantly denied that they were consciously trying to remember such things as spellings, punctuation, or any special textual organisations or arrangements. On the contrary, the many interviews we had with these children clearly demonstrated that they had a **'meaning' focus**. They were conscious of trying to remember the names (or events or happenings). They were not conscious of having ever deliberately focused on many of the text features which were found in their retellings. While we found this interesting, we did not realise initially how significant these facts were.

Secondly, we noticed that many of those text features (i.e. those on which the children claimed they were not consciously focusing) were finding their way into other writing these children were doing, sometimes a considerable time after the actual retelling had taken place. These text features ran the whole spectrum — words, phrases, ideas, rhetorical devices, organisation of content, as well as relatively superficial things such as spelling, punctuation marks and setting out. When questioned about this, in many instances the children were not consciously aware of where any of these particular text features had come from. This we hadn't expected, especially the way in which some features persevered over time. We decided to call this phenomenon **'delayed spillover'**.

On pages 20 and 21 are two texts. One, 'The Lone Dog', was used as a text for a retelling session in May of the school year. The other, 'Death Alley', was a text which Neill Paxton, a grade 5 pupil, began drafting in late June and completed in September of that year.

If you read each carefully, you will detect certain structural and semantic similarities within them which stretch the bounds of coincidence to the limit. Both pieces establish rather bleak, inhospitable settings for the plot to unfold, with swirling leaves and litter being integral parts of the setting. Both involve a struggle for survival. Night and darkness are used in both pieces to increase the intensity of the mood. The main characters are both sick, injured, helpless, and near to death. Both take something which has a physical effect which is described ('milk swelled his sides' and 'drugs filled his body'). When interviewed about the evolution of 'Death Alley', Neil originally maintained that he 'made it all up himself'. When we took him back through the reading and writing he'd done, he became aware of the subtle influences that the original retelling piece had had on his later writing.

The Lone Dog

Athina Barkirtzidoy

The wind blew fiercely, picking up leaves and dust as it swept down the street. Then out of a corner came a little dog, staggering as he went, and blinking dust out of his eyes. He felt weak and very hungry because he had not eaten that day. In fact it was not very often that he could find a scrap to eat.

He collapsed under a doorstep, struggling to get up. His legs ached and his eyes strained to see clearly against the wind. It was pitch black for a moment. Suddenly a very bright light shone right into the dog's face. Dazzled, he could not see who was speaking.
'Lisa,' a voice came from nowhere, 'Lisa, come quickly.'

The dog was now completely unconscious and did not know what was happening around him. He was lifted up by a gentle old man and his grand-daughter Lisa. 'Is it alive?' she asked, almost choking on her words. 'I think so,' replied the old man. 'But anyway, let's put a warm rug by the fireplace.'

The dog awoke next morning looking around with wide eyes. The one thing which he noticed most was the smell of warm food—which he had never tasted in his life. Just then Lisa came into the room carrying a bowl of warm milk. Unsure whether to try it or not, the dog dipped his muzzle into the bowl. One taste told him it was the best thing he had ever eaten. He drank quickly. The milk swelled his sides, giving him a warm feeling he had never known before.

The dog slowly staggered to his feet and looked at the girl. She seemed friendly but he had seen others like her who were very cruel indeed. He put his muzzle towards her and licked her hand. Lisa patted his shiny back and stroked his ears smoothly.
'What will we call him, Grandpa?' she asked. Her grandfather thought for a while. 'Stanley? Do you like Stanley for a name?'
'No!' Lisa said. 'Pepie would suit him better.'
'Yes,' said Grandpa. 'Pepie it is!'
And from that day to this, Pepie still lives happily with Grandpa and Lisa.

Feather or Fur, Young Australia Basic Reader 9, Nelson 1982

Death Alley

Neill Paxton (5th grade)

It was a cold harsh night and the wind was strong, blowing furiously through the never-ending alleys. It tossed up leaves and litter and turned them over with the least bit of care. This cycle took place time after time. Suddenly silence broke and there was a clash of garbage tins. A shadow covered the alley and a figure stumbled into sight. He huddled up into a corner of the alley. Slowly he raised the syringe into the air and gazed at it. With the most delicate touch the needle pierced the skin and drugs soon filled his body. As the street lights flickered he struggled to his feet. He followed the wall that was marked with graffiti. The night was long and the night was cold but the man fought for his life. Death was close and the rain pelted down on the garbage tins. The man crawled across the alley and paused for a while. The rain stopped and the man slowly stopped breathing.

Sly Old Fox

by Chelsea Cappetta

Once there was a sly old fox who loved plump juicy chickens for his meals. One morning he found a large opening in the chicken wire on a farmers farm. It was a bit high for chickens to get out but just right for very hungry foxes. So he crept inside, took a plump chicken and ran away to eat it. Next day the fox jumped though the wire grabbed a chicken and hurried away. This went on for days and days. All of a sudden, no more chickens. Then the fox grew thin and died. That taught him a lesson.

MORAL: Take all, Lose all.

This is another example of delayed spillover. It is one of three fables rewritten by Chelsea three weeks after doing the original retelling.

The degree and variety of delayed spillover intrigued us. There were too many examples for it to be attributed to chance. We feel reasonably secure in asserting that what we were observing was causally related to the retelling experience.

How to Explain Linguistic Spillover

If these children were telling us the truth (and the evidence is clear that they were), how could they internalise, without apparent effort, aspects of text to which they were not consciously attending? How could they attend to the meanings and put away in memory such details as spellings, uses of punctuation, phrases, vocabulary and other accoutrements of text structure, which they could draw on and employ later? While we cannot offer a full explanation of the phemonemon of linguistic spillover yet, we believe the following factors will contribute to an understanding of what is actually taking place when learners engage in the kinds of written retellings we asked them to do:
• the relationship between reading, writing, talking and listening
• how language is learned
• retelling as a 'natural' form of language behaviour
• retelling and conscious awareness of language details.

The Relationship between Reading, Writing, Listening, Talking

What we observed strongly supports the notion that the tradition of fragmenting language into four so-called language arts (i.e. reading, writing, listening, talking) is, as far as learning is concerned, a quite arbitrary and artificial separation. On the contrary, our observations of linguistic spillover are best supported by the theoretical view that language is a single, unitary process, manifesting itself through a range of different, but essentially parallel, forms. The essence of the relationship between language modes is encapsulated in a visual metaphor by Harste, Burke and Woodward, in a recent publication (HBW, 1983).

Linguistic Data Pool

Reading encounter	DATA POOL	Reading
Writing encounter		Writing
Speaking encounter		Speaking
Listening encounter		Listening

Harste, Burke, & Woodward, 1979

We've interpreted this metaphor thus: All language learners have an ever-increasing pool of knowledge about language (i.e. a 'data pool') somewhere inside their heads. This data pool is continually being added to from a variety of sources. When one is engaged in a reading encounter, for example, one is not only learning about something which can be labelled 'reading', one is also adding to one's data pool knowledge about vocabulary, about the way texts are structured, words are spelt, how various forms of punctuation are used, and a host of other items about language and how it is used. Once in the data pool this knowledge can be drawn upon when engaged in some other kind of language encounter, for example, writing. Listening and talking encounters also feed into and draw from this data pool. So the vocabulary encountered while listening to someone talk may eventually find its way into the data pool, to be drawn upon when reading at some later date, or perhaps when writing some months later. Similarly, the kinds of things read about may be drawn on when listening to someone talk.

How Language is Learned

Our observations that children internalise a wide range of text features as a result of regularly taking part in the retelling procedure can also be partially explained by some newer, emerging views of learning which are dramatically different from traditional views. While there have been many different theories of learning developed over the last century, essentially they have at their core the same logic. It goes something like this:

- Learning is essentially habit formation.
- The degree of learning which occurs is related to the concept of habit strength.
- Habit strength is a function of the strength of the association between a stimulus and a response.
- The stronger the association, the stronger the habit.
- Repetition of stimulus and response increases strength of association.

When applied to teaching the so-called language arts, this view of learning has two direct consequences. First, it results in an emphasis on repetition (practice) of desirable or good habits. This means many conscious repetitions of stimulus-response patterns, usually of fragments of language ('practice makes perfect'). Second, it means the identification and rooting out of incipient bad habits (mistakes or errors) before they become fixed.

This view of learning simply cannot explain the kinds of learning which we were observing as a consequence of our retelling sessions. It was obvious, for example, that many of the text features which had been learned by our children were not being repeated (i.e. 'strongly associated'). Furthermore, the learners were not conscious of deliberately setting out to learn or practise any specific aspects of the texts which they were being asked to retell.

We believe that what we observed could be better explained within the framework of what has become known as 'natural learning'. This view of learning argues essentially that learning to control the written form of the language ought not to be any more difficult, or less successful, than learning to control the oral form, **as long as the same conditions apply.** These conditions have been written about extensively elsewhere (Cambourne, 1987(a)). A summary of these conditions and how they interact with each other is shown on page 26.

The retelling procedure which our learners regularly experienced was characterised by many of these conditions. Our learners were being immersed in texts, in which a multiplicity of text features was demonstrated. There were high expectations that they would engage with these texts and the text features, but the responsibility for those which they did eventually engage with was left to the learners. They did approximate both the full set of meanings and many of the text features which were contained in what they read and retold. They did receive responses which both supported them and provided feedback and information. Finally, they were obviously employing — in very functional ways — language in its four basic forms (reading, writing, listening, talking).

Just as these conditions explain how very young children learn to control the oral form of the language of their culture, they can help to explain the kinds of learning we observed during the retelling sessions.

The Retelling Procedure as a 'Natural' Form of Language Behaviour

We strongly suspect that one of the reasons for the learning which we observed can be found in the nature of the retelling task itself. It's not a new form of behaviour which has to be learned. 'Telling about' what has happened (recounting or narrating what took place) is a well established form of linguistic behaviour. In the ebb and flow of everyday verbal encounters, speakers spend a great deal of time on the theme: 'This is an event (experience, etc.) which I want to share.' Next time you're in the staffroom at recess time listen to what your colleagues do with language. They spend a lot of time sharing 'what happened'— what happened in the TV show they watched last night; what happened in the book they read; what happened in their classroom; what happened at the party they went to, and so on.

The function and form of 'telling about' is a long-established feature of most people's verbal repertoires. It's not a new language form which they have to master. Because of this, learners are comfortable with retelling. They know how to do it, because they've been doing it for years. The most frequent kind of 'telling about what happened' is between close associates and/or acquaintances. Thus, there is little potential for stress or anxiety, and when anxiety is reduced, the capacity for learning is increased.

THE CONDITIONS OF LEARNING:
(A schematic representation of Brian Cambourne's model of learning as they apply to literacy learning)

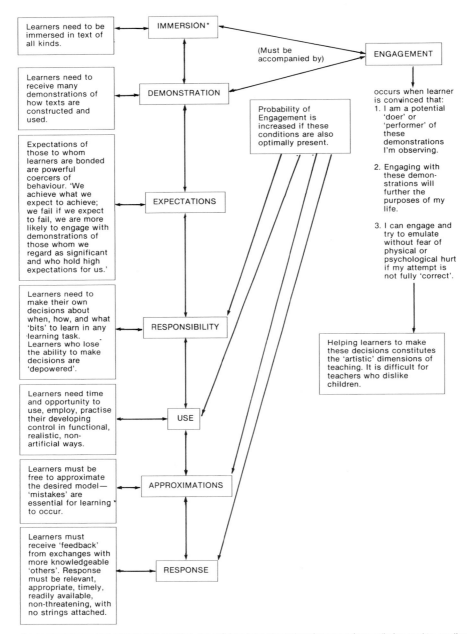

Learners need to be immersed in text of all kinds.

IMMERSION*

(Must be accompanied by)

ENGAGEMENT

Learners need to receive many demonstrations of how texts are constructed and used.

DEMONSTRATION

Probability of Engagement is increased if these conditions are also optimally present.

occurs when learner is convinced that:
1. I am a potential 'doer' or 'performer' of these demonstrations I'm observing.

2. Engaging with these demonstrations will further the purposes of my life.

Expectations of those to whom learners are bonded are powerful coercers of behaviour. 'We achieve what we expect to achieve; we fail if we expect to fail, we are more likely to engage with demonstrations of those whom we regard as significant and who hold high expectations for us.'

EXPECTATIONS

3. I can engage and try to emulate without fear of physical or psychological hurt if my attempt is not fully 'correct'.

Learners need to make their own decisions about when, how, and what 'bits' to learn in any learning task. Learners who lose the ability to make decisions are 'depowered'.

RESPONSIBILITY

Helping learners to make these decisions constitutes the 'artistic' dimensions of teaching. It is difficult for teachers who dislike children.

Learners need time and opportunity to use, employ, practise their developing control in functional, realistic, non-artificial ways.

USE

Learners must be free to approximate the desired model — 'mistakes' are essential for learning to occur.

APPROXIMATIONS

Learners must receive 'feedback' from exchanges with more knowledgeable 'others'. Response must be relevant, appropriate, timely, readily available, non-threatening, with no strings attached.

RESPONSE

'Immersion' means that prior to this retelling, the children have, through various experiences (being read to, reading themselves, discussion, various writing/sharing activities), been given the opportunity to become familiar with the concepts, language, structure, etc. of the retelling theme. Thus if it is a myth being retold, they have been immersed in other myths prior to this one being retold. If the topic is rainforests, the concepts inherent therein have been presented through other texts, experiences, prior to the retelling text being used.

The Retelling Procedure and Conscious Awareness of Language

The retelling procedure, as we define it, coerces learners to bring to their conscious awareness many features of text structure on which they would not typically focus, or upon which they would not typically reflect. This coercion is a consequence of not only having to read the texts which they eventually retell, but also of having to share and compare their retellings with others. This leads to much discussion about text and text features. This discussion ('sharing and comparing') means that many text characteristics and text relationships, which would normally remain implicit if one merely read and didn't retell and share, are made explicit.

Many researchers and thinkers in the field have argued that becoming consciously aware of the relationships that exist within and between texts is fundamental to learning to understand and control the written form of the language. Smith (1981) describes how the learner-writer needs to come to an understanding of 'the inner workings of the written language system'. Halliday (1986) has referred to the necessity of 'pulling up from one's linguistic guts all that one knows about oral language in order to understand and learn written language'.

We believe that the retelling procedure maximises the probability that learners will become consciously aware of text in ways that would not occur if they only read and didn't engage in retelling.

Summary

The retelling procedure as defined in this book maximises the potential for the four most common forms of language behaviour (reading, writing, talking, listening) to be used together in ways that mutually support and develop each other. Furthermore, it coerces learners not only to focus on meaning, but to recreate meaning, and to discuss and reflect upon those meanings which are being created. In the course of this reflection, learners cannot but fail to have brought to their conscious awareness the precise nature of the relationships between these four modes of language and the processes involved in creating texts when using any or all of them. The processes which underpin the typical retelling session simulate those conditions of learning which have been identified as necessary for successful language learning.

3

The 'What', 'How' and 'Why' of the Retelling Procedure

How many kinds of retelling procedures are there? How does one go about setting up the conditions for the retelling procedure to achieve its maximum effect? Are there any steps or stages of a typical retelling session? Is there an inflexible 'recipe' which must be followed? What does a typical retelling session look like? These and other questions will be addressed in this chapter.

The Range and Variety of Retelling Procedures

Two positive features of the retelling procedure that teachers like are that it is:
- suitable for a whole range of language abilities
- flexible in its use.

It is important that teachers who plan to use the retelling procedure as a regular language learning activity should appreciate and understand how it can be varied to accommodate different levels of language ability or to meet the different language learning purposes they may have. A good place to begin is with some of the different forms which the retelling procedure can take.

Different Forms of the Retelling Procedure

There are four general forms and two sub-categories of the retelling procedure:

1. One can listen to a teacher tell or read aloud a text and then retell it orally. We have called this 'oral-to-oral retelling'.

   This form of retelling can be used with non-readers or non-writers.

It can also be used to gain insights into learners' listening skills and/or their degree of control over oral forms of the language.

2(a). One can listen to a teacher tell or read aloud a text and then retell it in writing. We have called this 'oral-to-written retelling'.

This form of retelling can be used with both immature and mature readers/writers. It can also be used to gain insight into learners' listening skills and/or degrees of control over the written forms of language.

2(b). This is a variation of oral-to-written retelling. One can listen to a teacher tell or read aloud a text and then retell it by drawing. We have called this 'oral-to-drawing-retelling'.

This can be used with non-readers/non-writers. If these students are allowed to talk about their drawings, one can gain insight into their listening comprehension and control of oral language.

3. One can read a text and then retell it orally. We have called this 'written-to-oral retelling'.

This form can be used with readers who perhaps have difficulty with, or a fear of, writing (e.g. Non-English speaking background (NESB) learners, and immature learners). It is useful for gaining insight into reading comprehension and degrees of control over the oral forms of language.

4(a). One can read a text and then retell it in writing. We have called this 'written-to-written retelling'.

This form can be used with learners who have some degrees of control over reading and writing. It is useful for gaining insight into the degree of reading power (i.e. comprehension) and control over the written forms of language.

4(b). This is a variation of written-to-written retelling. One can read a text and retell it by drawing. We have called this 'written-to-drawing retelling'.

This form is useful with learners who can read but have difficulty with, or a fear of, writing. If learners are subsequently encouraged to talk about their drawings, teachers can gain insight into reading comprehension and degree of control over oral language forms.

Because this book is aimed at the primary school child it focuses on the written-to-written retelling procedure, i.e. Category 4. However, once teachers have used and come to understand what this form of the retelling procedure is all about, they will be able to shift from form to form as the context, purpose, or pupil level of language development changes.

Establishing Classroom Conditions to Ensure the Retelling Procedure Succeeds

When we first began experimenting with the retelling procedure we found that not all children were enamoured with the sessions we put them through. They told us such things as:

- 'It was boring.'
- 'I was frightened that I wouldn't be able to remember everything.'
- 'There was just too much to write down and I got sick of it.'
- 'I don't like just trying to write down someone else's story.'

These experiences were sometimes repeated when we tried to explain the procedure to fellow teachers at workshops. We remember vividly the teacher who, after doing a written retelling of Thurber's *The Scotty Who Knew Too Much* (see Chapter 1), announced: 'That was really boring and difficult. I was so busy trying to rote memorise the story that I thought I was back in secondary school preparing for an exam. This procedure would go down like a lead balloon with my year fives.'

We realised that retellings done under conditions which produced such negative responses were definitely not conducive to learning. We obviously needed to develop a learning context which produced quite different perceptions of the purposes and functions of the retelling procedure. So, we asked ourselves what were the characteristics of a learning setting in which learners readily and willingly engage, for an extended period, with complex tasks which they seem to enjoy, and to which they willingly keep returning? We found that there were plenty of examples in the world: learning to play complex games, learning to make friends, learning to talk, and so on. These activities seemed to have certain common features:

- they usually involve social interaction with others who are friendly, supportive, understanding, accepting and caring;
- they are unpressured, non-anxious situations;
- participants always understand the purposes and functions of the activities which occur in the setting;
- participants clearly and unambiguously know the appropriate role to adopt in the setting;
- participants perceive the activities which occur in the settings to be relevant to their needs and purposes;
- participants feel safe about taking part in the activities in the setting without fear of being hurt, ridiculed, denigrated or demeaned if they make mistakes.

We realised that it would be necessary to establish similar conditions in the retelling session. **However, we found that when we attempted to do so we were forced to establish a climate which spread well beyond the confines of the retelling session and spilled over into our whole approach to teaching and learning language.**

For example, friendly, supportive, caring, social interaction cannot be turned on just for retelling sessions, while for the rest of the day the class is expected to sit up, shut-up, and listen to the teacher, and compete with each other. Unpressured, non-anxious situations are impossible when learners feel that their performance is being judged and/or compared unfavourably against some set of norms. Participants cannot feel safe about having a go at the activities of the setting if they know their performance is going to be judged and that attention will be drawn to their errors and/or weaknesses.

Similarly, when we tried to give our students an understanding of the purposes and functions of the retelling procedure, which they could perceive as relevant to their needs and purposes, we found that we ranged far beyond the boundaries of the actual retelling lesson. For example, we told our students that the major purpose/function of retellings was to help them with their learning, their writing and their reading. We explained that if they participated in the ways we demonstrated, they would get ideas to help them with their writing and for achieving special effects, and they would learn about interesting things and would improve their reading.

If learners are going to accept these rather simple justifications they must be in classrooms in which reading, writing and learning are valued and held in high esteem. This can only happen if the learners are given repeated demonstrations from a 'significant other' (i.e. someone they like and who likes them) that highlight the value and importance of being a reader and writer.

In other words, for the retelling procedure to have a remote chance of working effectively, the classroom climate must be that of the whole-language/natural learning classroom.*

What Does This Mean for Implementing the Retelling Procedure?

It means that if teachers want to maximise the textual learning that will take place through the retelling procedure they need to be aware of the principles upon which the whole-language/natural learning philosophy is based. Not only do they need to understand them, but they need to be able to implement them.

This is not to say that the retelling procedure will not work in classrooms which are not 'perfect' exemplars of the whole-language/natural learning philosophy. In fact, we don't believe that there is any such perfect classroom. The research carried out in the last few years into teachers' interpretations of what a whole-language/natural learning philosophy means, shows quite unequivocally that there are many valid interpretations of this philosophy (Cambourne & Turbill, 1987; Cambourne, 1987(b)).

We also believe that the most important factors in the success or failure of the retelling procedure are affective and attitudinal rather than methodological. **By this, we mean that what teachers do to help the children in their classes develop positive self-concepts as learners, readers and writers is of more importance than the actual methods employed.**

---

*This is not the appropriate place for giving full details of the 'whole-language/natural learning' approach. More information can be found in Cambourne, B. L., *Natural Learning and Literacy Education*, Ashton-Scholastic, 1987.

It just so happens that the whole-language/natural learning philosophy is based on methods which ensure that positive self-concepts and attitudes are developed. In essence, the classroom climate in which the retelling procedure will be most effective as a language developer will be one which has all or most of the characteristics of the optimal learning settings described above, namely:

- they usually involve social interaction with others who are friendly, supportive, understanding, accepting and caring;
- they are 'unpressured', 'non-anxious' situations;
- participants always understand the purposes and functions of the activities which occur in the setting;
- participants clearly, and unambiguously, know the appropriate role to adopt in the setting;
- participants perceive the activities which occur in the settings to be relevant to their needs and purposes;
- participants feel safe about taking part in the activities in the setting without fear of being hurt, ridiculed, denigrated, or demeaned if they make mistakes.

Classrooms which rank high on these conditions will be suitable contexts for implementing the retelling procedure as we've designed it.

What Actually Happens in a Retelling Session?

An effective way of illustrating how these principles can be applied in the context of a retelling session is to present a pen-picture of the retelling procedure being implemented in a classroom. In what follows, we present a case study of a typical retelling session, reconstructed from video records, with explanatory comments. But, first, here is a lesson plan of the retelling session so that you can get an overall picture.

LESSON PLAN

Preparation
(Immersion in genre and topic. This immersion takes place in the days or weeks prior to the actual retelling session.)
(a) Class organised into groups of 4–5 students.
(b) Text chosen and multiple copies made.
(c) Copies folded so that only title is visible.

Part 1—Predicting (5–10 minutes)

(a) **Predict a Plot.** On the basis of the title (which is the only part visible) each member of the class is asked to write one or two sentences on what a story with such a title *might* be about. Students should work quickly (two minute maximum). Spelling, and neatness is of secondary/minor importance.

(b) **Predict Some Words**. If the prediction you make turned out to be what the story is about, list some words/phrases which you would expect to encounter (two minute maximum). (See footnote on page 00.)

(c) **Share and Compare**. Each student may read aloud what they've written for (a) and (b) above (one minute maximum).

(d) **Make a Comment**. Each person is to make one comment (orally) on the written predictions of one other member of his/her group. Everyone else should listen (three minutes).

Part 2—Everyone Read

In this section literally everybody reads. Firstly the teacher reads aloud, while the children listen. It is important that the children receive demonstrations of how the text sounds when read by an expert reader. Every such demonstration adds to their linguistic data pools. After the teacher has read orally, everybody reads the text silently. Teachers should continually expound the following points:
(a) One can read the text as many times as one needs to. The aim is to feel confident and comfortable with the meanings in it.
(b) The aim is *not* to rote memorise; the aim *is to understand*.
(c) When one understands something recall is easy. When one tries to rote memorise special points, retellings are hard.
   During this part of the session, it is legitimate to explain the specific purposes of the retelling (if there are any). This is because the purpose for retelling can significantly affect how the text is read. For example, if the purpose of the retelling was to 'retell the text for someone who was not familiar with it, so that they could enjoy it as much as you did', the reading strategies employed would be different from when the purpose was to 'retell the main ideas only'.

Part 3—Retell (10–15 minutes)

In this case, it is a written retelling (oral retellings are also a possibility). Here are the directions which are given.
(a) Turn over the sheet that the story is printed on, and write out your recall for someone else who hasn't read the story. (See part 2 above.)
(b) Do not look back to the story.
(c) Do not worry about neatness or spelling. The most important thing is that it is readable by you.
(d) Work as quickly as you can.

Part 4—Share and Compare

(a) **How Are Our Retellings Different**? Find a partner and ask each other:
   • 'What did I include/omit that is different to what you included/omitted?'
   • 'Why did you omit this bit?'

(b) **Muddled-Meanings**. Everybody ask his/her partner: 'Do you think I muddled-up, changed, or omitted anything that alters meaning?'

(c) **Paraphrase Power**. Everybody ask his/her partner: 'Did you use any words/phrases that are different from those in the story but still mean the same thing?'

(d) **Borrow a Bit**. Everybody ask his/her partner: 'If you could take a bit of my retelling and include it in yours, which bit would you take? Why?'

A Case Study of the Retelling Procedure in Action

Let us take the lesson plan set out above and clearly separate and explain the different teaching/learning steps. The various phases are explained, each followed by the rationale (set in italics).

RETELLING PROCEDURE: A TIME-LINE OF TEACHING/LEARNING ACTIVITIES

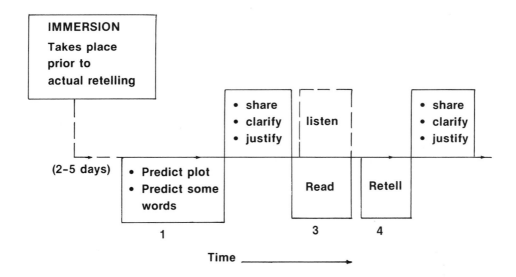

We will now follow this retelling session with a Grade 5 class through the sequence of events on the time-line.

PRE-TELLING SESSION PHASE: Immersion

The retelling text for this session was entitled 'Preserve Our Rainforests'. It was the third retelling text to be attempted in a theme entitled 'Rainforests'. During the previous two weeks the teacher had attempted to immerse the children in the concepts and details associated with rainforests. She'd done this by:

- conducting 'shared-book' lessons, with texts on rainforests. These texts were mainly expository and dealt with such concepts as the location of rainforests, the conditions necessary for location, and the plants and animals found in rainforests.
- providing books and materials on the topic for children to choose during the compulsory sustained silent reading time (SSR) which occurred every day.
- by talking herself (and encouraging the children to talk) about what they'd been reading (during SSR) and what they'd heard her reading (during shared-book time).
- by occasionally encouraging the children to brainstorm orally and list everything they thought they'd learnt about the topic, with a partner.
- by conducting two previous retelling procedures using a text entitled *Inhabitants of the Rainforest* and a diagrammatic representation of the layers of a rainforest. The first of these was an expository, descriptive piece and the second piece was the diagram which children had to transform (i.e. 'retell') in verbal form. These two retelling sessions had provoked a great deal of talk and discussion about rainforests.

It should be remembered that these children had been told that retellings, if done in the right spirit, would help them with their learning, reading and writing, and would quite often supply ideas for future writing. It should also be remembered that these children were in a classroom climate where learning, reading and writing were highly valued and esteemed.

RATIONALE

Successful retellings can only occur if the potential retellers can devote most of their cognitive energy and memory space to the construction of meaning. Texts which contain foreign or unknown concepts are not as predictable as those which contain few new concepts or little strange vocabulary. Readers or listeners who are confronted with concepts and vocabulary which is unfamiliar become anxious and are therefore placed under pressure. Reading behaviour changes when pressure and anxiety increase. Readers who are unsure of the concepts which they are reading about begin to attempt to rote memorise the text. When this happens, linguistic spillover stops and learners develop negative attitudes towards the retelling procedure.

Familiarity with the subject matter, promoted by lots of talk and discussion, builds confidence in the learner's control of meanings. Confidence leads to increased readiness to tackle the text in future encounters. Talk and discussion also sensitise children to their peers' points of view, and their strengths and weaknesses. Such sensitivity leads to caring and tolerance of others in the group.

RETELLING PHASE (a) Introduction to Session

This is what the teacher said when she introduced this retelling session: 'The retelling for today is still on the topic of rainforests. You already know a great deal about rainforests because you've done so much reading and talking about the topic. This retelling is slightly different from the others. Who'll volunteer to tell us, in list form, all the things they know about rainforests?'

Natasha volunteered and gave an oral list of about 12 items of knowledge. The teacher praised Natasha's efforts.

RATIONALE

*Learners need to be reassured that they do have the background knowledge and the confidence to attempt the task. The invitation for volunteers to contribute by giving an oral list is important. Freedom **not** to volunteer to perform reduces the pressure that accompanies forced performance and thus increases confidence. The act of hearing someone else brainstorm the list helps to reactivate each child's own background knowledge, and begins to give the appropriate mental set to the rest of the group. Furthermore, hearing another's list helps some of the slower, less able learners to 'narrow down', i.e. it gives them a workable focus.*

Telling the group 'this one is slightly different' rather than telling them explicitly 'this is an argumentative, persuasive text' alerts them to the possibility of difference but doesn't produce anxiety about the meanings of 'argumentative' or 'persuasive'. This will be made explicit later when participants attempt to reconstruct the text. Engagement with notions like 'argumentative' and 'persuasive' is likely to be higher after attempting to write an argumentative or persuasive text.

(b) Predict a Plot

The teacher then handed out the texts, folded so that only the title 'Preserve our Rainforests' was visible. She then said to the group: 'Do you think this is going to be fiction or non-fiction? (She read the title.) On the basis of the title what do you think it will be about? Write no more than two sentences on what you think a text with that title might be about. Don't worry about spelling or neatness. You're the only one who's going to read it.'

At this point the children sat quietly as if contemplating the possibilities inherent in the title. After a few moments, they began to write. The teacher watched them carefully. When the first of them seemed to have run out of ideas for predicting a plot, she moved into the next part of the lesson:

(c) Predict Some Words

'While you're waiting for the others to finish, see if you can predict some words which might be in a text with that title.'* One by one the children set about doing the list.

---

*Since this session we have decided to instruct children specifically to brainstorm as long a list as possible in a minute. However, in this session the instruction was interpreted by the children as three or four words.

RATIONALE

Predicting serves a number of purposes. First, it is basic to the reading process, and practice at doing it and then comparing the prediction with the actual text highlights the relationships between the title and the possible and the actual text. Second, we have observed that readers will engage more deeply with a text after predicting its content. The children tell us they like to see how close their predictions were.

Third, predicting at a number of levels is important. In this lesson the children were asked to predict at the whole-text level, at the genre level (fiction/non-fiction) and at the word level. All these predictions lead to deeper engagement with important aspects of the text. The discussion which flows from these predictions provides the opportunity for bringing to conscious awareness such concepts as text-structure and the differences between fiction and non-fiction, as well as the meanings of a whole range of words. Brainstorming a list of possible words gives a mental set, and is a kind of revision and/or recall of the immersion which has been going on.

(d) Sharing the Predictions

The teacher waited until the children finished their predictions (see footnote on page 36) and then invited volunteers to share their predictions.

Teacher: 'Who'd like to share their predictions with the rest of the group?'

Chelsea: 'I predicted it would be about people who want to keep the rainforests of Australia. The words I predicted were "save", "conditions" and "rainforest".'

Teacher: 'Why would you predict those things?'

Chelsea: 'Because "preserve" means to save and on the TV I heard about them trying to stop the logging of rainforest in Tasmania.'

Teacher: 'Would anyone like to comment on Chelsea's predictions?'

In what followed, Leanne agreed with Chelsea for similar reasons (knowledge of the meaning of 'preserve' and family experiences of bushwalking and a concern for the environment). The teacher enthusiastically praised the plausibility and sense of all of the predictions. Branco then volunteered a comment.

Branco: 'I wasn't really sure about "preserve" but I knew it had something to do with things that had been there a long time.'

Le-Minh and Phillip, the other two members of the group, did not volunteer to share or comment.

RATIONALE

The emphasis is still on volunteering. Allowing for voluntary sharing permits confidence to develop. Confidence is directly related to the degree to which a learner feels in control of what is being learned. Notice how the teacher accepted and praised each volunteered set of predictions. She knew how important it was in retelling procedure for those who participate to know and understand that speculation is not only permitted, but is highly valued.

Notice too how the teacher asked Chelsea to justify her predictions. Making explicit the reasons for statements is important for the development of 'meta-textual awareness' (i.e. conscious awareness of the process/options one has available for solving meaning-related problems.)

Finally, the whole process of sharing predictions opens up for each participant a variety of ideas and speculation about texts and meanings. The sharings provide demonstrations or models of speculation and the creation of meaning.

(e) Reading the Text

The teacher read the text through while the children followed on their copies.

Preserve Our Rainforest

Two hundred years ago Australia had large expanses of rainforest — lush areas of tall, densely packed trees — home to many unusual creatures.

However, the early settlers who followed Captain Cook, cleared and destroyed vast sections of this rainforest. They cleared land so that they could farm, run cattle and grow crops. They also destroyed much rainforest by logging the rich, red cedar trees which were wanted by furniture makers. Gradually our rainforest started to disappear — now there is not very much left.

Australia must realise that the rainforest which remains must be preserved; clearing for farming and logging for timber must stop now before all our rainforest is destroyed. Many animals need the rainforest to survive; the cuscus and tree kangaroo live only in rainforest. What will happen to them if we don't stop the destruction of our jungles? The government should preserve all rainforest as national parks so that all Australians, now and in the future, may enjoy their beauty.

Teacher: 'Now you can read it as many times as you need to, then when you're confident that you understand it, turn it over and retell the text in your own words.'

The children found a quiet section of the room and proceeded to read and re-read the texts silently.

RATIONALE

The teacher read the text first. As well as helping the less proficient reader over hurdles in the text, this gives all participants added confidence to hear the text interpreted orally by the teacher—the acknowledged expert.

The children are given the freedom to read and re-read the text until confident they understand it. It is important that children do not perceive retelling as a testing procedure. Rather they must see it as an important non-threatening opportunity to learn and develop skills in something which is valued, esteemed and relevant. The number of times that children will re-read a text will vary from child to child and from genre to genre. The threads which hold fictional writing together are very different from those which are used in expository text. Children need to read as often or as slowly as suits them in order to maximise comprehension.

(f) The Written Retelling

When they decided that they were confident they understood the text, the children turned it over, opened their books and began to write. Some, of course, finished before others. When the teacher noticed this she said: 'While you're waiting for the others, proofread your retelling text. If you finish that, find something to read or finish some contract work.'

RATIONALE

Children need all the time necessary to get their retelling right. The instruction to proofread coerces a closer inspection of their own text, and a consideration of the conventions which they will eventually need to control.

(g) Share and Compare

When the children appeared to have finished their retellings, the teacher called them together for the final phase of the lesson.
Teacher: 'It's time to share and compare our retellings. I want you to listen carefully because I might call on you to respond. Remember, you must give a reason for any statements you make and you must be constructive.'
Then to no one in particular, she said: 'How did you find that piece of writing? Was it difficult or easy? Why?'
Chelsea: 'Easy, because we've been learning about rainforests, and logging is really topical at the moment. Would you like to hear mine?' Chelsea reads hers.

9.7.86.   *Preserve our rainforest*

I think this writing is going to be about people who want to keep the rainforests of Australia.

save conditions rainforest.

Many year ago (at the time when Captain Cook discovered the east coast), ther used to be

more rainforest. After Captain Cook people
cut down our rainforest for wood.
If no rainforests are left where will all the nature
of Australia be? Will anybody in the future see
one? No probaly not. Cuscus and tree kangaroo
only have rainforest as their home. Will they
survive? No probaly not. How would you like it
if you were about to have no home just beca
use someone needs wood? Would you like
it. Of course not so fight!

'SAVE OUR RAINFOREST?'

After listening to Chelsea's retelling Branco challenged her interpretation.
Branco: 'That was a thorough retelling, Chelsea, but you didn't say how long ago the destruction started.'
Chelsea: 'I did. I said "at the time when Cook discovered Australia" and that means 200 years ago because Cook discovered Australia in 1788.'

Phillip and Le-Minh also commented but added nothing new.
Phillip: 'I like your retelling, Chelsea, you've remembered to put everything in. It's similar to mine but you've used better words.'
Le-Minh: 'Chelsea's is like mine, but she said it in a different way.'

The children then shared and compared their text with one of their partners. They looked for things like muddled meanings, changes in emphasis, or good paraphrase. There was no compulsion for them to share any of their discussion with the rest of the group, but they often reported on some aspect of their own or their partner's text which intrigued them. Occasionally, the teacher invited these to be made public: 'That's really interesting, Phillip. Stop what you're doing, everyone, and listen to the paraphrase which Phillip found in Chelsea's retelling. Tell them about it, Phillip.'

Phillip did so and the teacher followed up with something like: 'Who else can recall a good paraphrase?' 'Why do you think it's a good one?' or 'How might you use that in your own writing?'

RATIONALE

This section of the lesson is where most of the opportunities occur for developing explicit knowledge of how texts work. This is where meta-textual awareness can be developed. Because all the students have attempted retelling, they can all learn about each others' interpretations of the same text. This means children can learn from their peers such things as:
- *there is more than one way to interpret a text*
- *the place and function of lead sentences and closure sentences*
- *the function of sequence in a text*

- *text/title relationships*
- *sub-heading/text relationships.*

Note also that while the voluntary nature of sharing in front of the whole group is maintained, group sharing is encouraged. Peer sharing, particularly in a supportive classroom, is less threatening because it's less public. Note also that all responses are accepted and given a positive comment somewhere. One of the purposes of this part of the lesson is to convince learners that their contributions are valued. The purpose is to avoid at all costs giving the message: "You blew it, kid, that's wrong."

Summary

The best and most enduring kind of learning occurs when children are placed in non-pressured situations, where the probability that experimentation will occur is significantly increased. The 'right to be wrong' and still be accepted is a very important aspect of the natural learning process. This is what enables young language learners to proceed from novice status to increasing levels of control over the oral form of language. Children need similar conditions when the written form of language is the focus.

What else do they need? They need to engage in purposeful activities which require them to think and to make decisions, to read and discuss, to justify and explain. They need to feel important and to be recognised and acknowledged when authentic effort and progress have been made. They need to feel part of a community of learners who can help or be helped, who will listen and respond constructively. They need stimulation and variety, resources and a forum in which learning is promoted. They need committed and caring teachers who are prepared to become participators (not merely facilitators) in the exciting world of learning.

How do teachers create this kind of world? First, it means lots of talk — spontaneous and undirected as well as structured. It requires continuous demonstrations and modelling of sensitive questioning techniques (always make a positive comment first). It means showing a genuine interest in the work and opinions of children, and maintaining a daily personal contact with each child, no matter how brief. It means sitting back and waiting for confidence to develop in oral sessions, so that what a child has to say is not 'forced'. It means permitting children to volunteer answers and responses. It means giving children the right **not** to share their work if they are not happy about it.

The retelling procedure fits best into this kind of environment. In such a learning context, retelling becomes a vehicle whereby reading and writing across the curriculum can be explored and developed. It is a powerful strategy for enabling children to transform a text into their own words, taking in what is only truly comprehended. By so doing, not only are they transforming information, they are unconsciously, and painlessly, learning to write in a particular genre, using style and sentence patterns, vocabulary, and all the other accoutrements of different forms of text.

4

Texts for Retelling

The texts included in this chapter have been specially chosen to give primary-aged children exposure to a comprehensive range of text types. They cover traditional children's literature, that which was originally told orally (myths, fables and fairy tales) because we believe these are a vital part of a child's literary development. They also include poetry in the form of free verse. It is a good genre for retelling as it coerces the child to read and interpret in the medium of imagery and word play. While it is possible that retelling of rhymed verse could be done, it is our experience that children get distracted by the rhyming pattern rather than concentrating on the meaning and imagery.

A section on Author Craft has been included later in this chapter. By this we mean the techniques authors use to achieve special purposes. The three special purposes highlighted are:

Setting — satisfactory description of the place within which the story or a major part of the action takes place.

Character — description of characters of importance; what they look like, how they act and speak and the ways in which other characters react towards them are important considerations.

Atmosphere — injection of mood and feeling, use of emotive language; it can be part of setting or character development. One child explained it as 'the use of light and dark words'.

From this base in narrative genre, a range of non-fiction texts which describe, persuade, argue, explain and instruct are presented. Children in primary school are in a dilemma, torn between pursuing the fiction books they love and the pressure of coming to terms with non-fiction books they know they need to read and will be expected to read more of in high school. In primary school, teachers are aware of this need to prepare their students for expository reading and writing, but all will tell of the difficulties of motivating children and of persuading them not to plagiarise text they often do not understand.

Read-and-retell is an excellent strategy to use in order to allow children to transform a text into their own words, taking only what is really understood. Not only are they retelling information, they are unconsciously and painlessly learning to write in a particular genre.

Several retellings are presented from diagrams, pictures and maps so that learners are forced to verbalise: to describe and interpret information from a different format.

We hope that these texts will provide a good base upon which teachers and children can build so that students are well prepared for high school, having widened their experience of written language and developed an understanding of the ways in which our language is used.

There are 38 texts in all which should adequately cover a four-term year. Some of the retellings are from well-known and loved children's authors such as Roald Dahl, E. B. White, Philippa Pearce and R. L. Stevenson. Other texts are actually fifth grade children's writing, evidence of the spillover effect mentioned earlier and of the internalisation of many aspects of narrative genre.

We hope that teachers will use this book, not as a collection of activities, but as a source of ideas upon which they can build to expand their children's literary awareness.

What Ages/Grades Can Use These Texts?

All 38 texts in this book have been tested with children in Grades 5 and 6 in the NSW primary school system in parallel classes. Their ages ranged from 9.5–12 years. We found that the children in these grades coped well with varying degrees of control and interpretation.

In addition, selected texts have been used successfully with children in Grades 3 and 4 (7.5–10 years). Narratives and descriptive text, diagrams and maps were handled very well by younger children.

Which Texts Should I Start With?

To help children become familiar with the procedures involved in retelling (defined earlier in this book) and, through familiarity to develop confidence and a sense of achievement, we recommend that teachers start the program with texts from traditional children's literature. Narratives such as fables, myths and fairy tales are already well known by most children. They have a reasonable grasp of the stylistic features of these stories and therefore such prose provides a strong medium through which to explore and develop the re-creation of meaning by retelling.

How Do I Plan for Retelling?

Timing
By trial and error we found that the retelling procedure was most effective when conducted over a three-week period. This allows several days for

immersion to occur with, say, three written retellings taking place in an 11–12 day period. We found that any longer than this was too demanding on both students and the teacher.

Variety and consolidation

We need to plan for variety in our language lessons: variety of text type and degree of difficulty of the retelling text. Each term needs a balance between fiction and non-fiction, between the more predictable and the less predictable, but each text must be given sufficient treatment and exposure to enable children to learn. For this reason we suggest that text types are programmed in sets of three and treated over a three-week period (see the sample, Year's Outline on page 45).

As most primary children read and write to a large extent in the fictional form, they find fictional retellings easier than non-fiction. Therefore, it is important to balance a term's program between fiction and non-fiction texts so that the children are presented with retellings of a wide range of difficulty. If texts are always presented at or above the perceived coping level of children, retelling would be pressured and onerous. Children need a challenge, but they can't take it constantly. To build the confidence to improve, we have to ensure that they are occasionally presented with texts they find easier to retell.

Once children have experienced certain text types via retelling, they should be encouraged to explore these further by reading, writing, sharing and comparing and by applying their knowledge. Brief ideas for consolidating and extending (or responding) may be found in this book along with the texts.

Layout

A simple programming format is provided in the Appendix and permission is given for teachers to use this if it satisfies their school requirements. It needs only one page of writing and at a glance will explain the text types involved, the purpose of the text and the time period of the program. It does not include evaluation. This is dealt with in more detail in Chapter 5. Included in that section is a suggested format for evaluation which is in accord with the NSW Writing Syllabus.

A YEAR'S OUTLINE

TERM 1

Fairy Tales
- 'The Frog Prince'
- 'The Real Princess'
- 'The Old Woman Who Lived in a Vinegar Bottle'

Fables
- 'The Goose and the Golden Eggs'
- 'The Wolf in Sheep's Clothing'
- 'The Mouse and the Bull'

Mysteries
- 'The Bermuda Triangle'
- 'Loch Ness Monster'

Read-do-Retell
- 'Pikelets'
- 'Roller Pattern'

TERM 2

Myths
- 'Why the Kangaroo Hops?'
- 'How Koalas Got Their Ears'
- 'How the Tiger Got Its Stripes'

Author Craft (developing character)
- 'My Father'
- 'Anne's Surprise'
- 'Long John Silver'

Expository text: Exploration
- 'Discovery of the Unknown East'
- 'Discovery of the Americas'
- 'Space: The New Frontier'
- 'Space Travel vs Famine Relief'

TERM 3

Author Craft (describing setting)
- 'The Barn'
- 'My Father's Garage'
- 'Aunt Gwen's House'

Poetry
- 'Fang'
- 'The Death of a Cat'
- 'The Sea Horse'

Diagrams:
Prehistoric Giants
- Barosaurus
- Torosaurus

Maps
- Australia/New Guinea
- South America

TERM 4

Author Craft (creating atmosphere)
- 'The Old Grey House'
- 'Death Alley'
- 'A Miserable Day'

Expository text:
Rainforests
- 'Rainforests'
- Rainforest Diagram
- 'Preserve Our Rainforest'

Diagrams
- The Water Cycle
- Life Cycle of Dragonfly

Traditional Children's Literature

Fables, fairy tales, myths

Text Type: Fables	Term: Weeks:

Purpose	• To allow children the opportunity to experiment/approximate the genre of fables as they re-create the text. • To allow children the opportunity to contemplate the value of moralising by telling a story. • To provide children with a focus and a forum to discuss and explore techniques used in fable writing.
Immersion (Teacher reading/child reading sharing discussion)	Children need many opportunities to listen to, and read, good examples of fables. Over 3–4 days the teacher should read a wide selection from Aesop and La Fontaine. Each reading session should be followed by discussion. Children should be encouraged to read and re-read collections of fables at school and at home, and to share their favourites.
Retelling	Using the standard procedure, retelling of the following texts occurs over a two-week period: • The Wolf in Sheep's Clothing • The Goose and the Golden Eggs • The Mouse and the Bull

Responding

1. Teacher-initiated discussion — small group or whole class — of the question 'What makes a fable a fable?'

2. Generated knowledge/criteria may be displayed on a wall chart.

3. Children should be encouraged to compare their knowledge with that published in a recognised authoritative source (such as an encyclopaedia).

4. Encourage children to use this knowledge as a basis for their own story writing.

The Wolf in Sheep's Clothing

There was once a wolf who grew tired of hunting for his food.

'It's such hard work and it's no fun being shot at by angry farmers,' he said.

So he thought of a clever plan. He decided to wrap himself in a sheepskin and live in a sheep pen. Then, when he grew hungry, he could kill a nice fat lamb for his dinner and not have to hunt to find it.

However, that same night the farmer also decided that he would like lamb for dinner and went down to the sheep pen. It was very dark and the farmer grabbed and killed the first sheep he found. Imagine his surprise when he found he had killed a wolf.

Moral: Never pretend to be someone else.

The Goose and the Golden Eggs

There was once a poor farmer and his wife who bought a goose. The next morning when the wife went into the farmyard she found that the goose had laid a golden egg. The husband and wife were delighted at their good fortune. Every morning they found a golden egg under the goose and soon they grew very rich. They had everything that money could buy and wanted for nothing.

However, the richer they became, the greedier they became. One day the farmer's wife spoke to her husband saying: 'One golden egg a day is not enough. We need more. If we kill the goose we can get all the gold inside her at once.'

So together they killed the goose that laid the golden eggs, but they found no gold. The goose was just like any other goose. The husband got angry with his wife, saying: 'Your greed has ruined us. Why couldn't you have been satisfied with one golden egg a day?'

Moral: Be thankful for what you've got.

The Mouse and the Bull

One day a mouse was playing in a farmer's field when he saw a large, black bull dozing nearby. Being a bit of a rascal, the mouse crept close to the huge animal and bit its tail. The bull roared and snorted and chased the little mouse around the farmyard. However, the tiny creature was too quick for the bull and hid in a hole in the wall. The bull charged at the wall time after time but nothing would move the little mouse safely hidden in the hole. Eventually, the bull was so exhausted that he sank to his knees, unable to go on any more.

Moral: The strong don't win every battle.

Text Type: Fairy Tales	Term: Weeks:

Purpose	• To allow children the opportunity to experiment/approximate the genre of fairy tales as they re-create the text. • To allow children the opportunity to contemplate the implicit messages of fairy tales. • To provide children with a focus and a forum to discuss and explore techniques used in writing fairy tales.

Immersion	Children should be provided with many opportunities to hear and read good examples of fairy tales. Over several days the teacher should read a wide selection and each reading session should be followed by discussion. Children should be encouraged to read and re-read collections of fairy tales at school and at home, and to share their favourites.

Retelling	Using the standard procedure, retelling of the following texts occur over a two-week period: • The Real Princess • The Frog Prince • The Old Woman Who Lived in a Vinegar Bottle

Responding

1. Teacher-initiated discussion — in small group or whole class — of the question 'What makes a fairy tale a fairy tale?'

2. Criteria for fairy tales may then be displayed on a chart and children asked to comment on the similarities and differences of fairy tales and fables.

3. Comparison of this knowledge can then be made by checking with the encyclopaedia.

4. Encourage children to use this knowledge as a basis for their own story writing.

The Real Princess

Once upon a time there was a prince, a very handsome prince, who wanted more than anything else to find and wed a real princess. So he travelled far and wide but nowhere could he find a girl of pure, royal blood. In despair he returned to live with his parents.

One dark and wintery evening they heard a tapping on the castle door and when the servants opened it they found a beautiful young girl who begged shelter for the night. On being brought before the royal family, the young girl announced herself as a princess.

'Oh, indeed,' thought the queen. 'We shall soon find out.'

She went to the bedchamber and placed a single green pea on the floor. On top of this she piled 20 mattresses and on top of those she piled 20 feather quilts. She then told the young girl to sleep there for the night.

The next morning the old queen hurried to find out how the girl had slept.

'Dreadfully,' she replied. 'The bed was so uncomfortable that my body is bruised and sore.'

The queen laughed and clapped her hands with joy for she knew that only a real princess would have so tender a skin as to feel a pea through twenty mattresses and twenty feather quilts.

The prince was also delighted and, after a short time he and the princess married and lived happily ever after.

The Frog Prince

Once upon a time there was a king who had three beautiful daughters and the youngest princess was the fairest of them all.

One day she went into the garden to play with her favourite toy, a perfect golden ball. She threw it high into the air and caught it, but it slipped through her fingers and rolled into a pond where it sank into the deep water.

'Oh, how will I ever get my lovely golden ball?' cried the princess. 'Who will help me find my golden ball?'

A slimy green frog jumped out of the water and croaked: 'I will, but in return let me be your companion and playmate, and live with you, eat from your plate, drink from your cup and sleep in your bed.'

The young princess, desperate to get her golden ball, quickly agreed. In the twinkling of an eye the frog had dived into the pool and retrieved the ball and laid it at her feet. Delighted, the girl skipped back to the castle and immediately forgot about the frog and the promises she had made.

The next day as the princess and her family sat at the great table eating dinner, they heard a splish, splash, splish, splash and a knocking at the door. The youngest princess opened the door and there sat the slimy frog, demanding that she keep the promise she had made by the pool. However, she wanted to forget that promise and slammed the door in the frog's face. The king, alarmed at the commotion, demanded to know the reason and the young princess told him the story of the golden ball and the frog.

'Well, my dear, if you made a promise then you must keep it,' said the king, and bade the princess open the door and let the frog in. The girl did as her father asked but cringed in horror and disgust as the frog sat on the table and ate food from her plate and drank from her cup.

At bedtime, the princess carried the frog with two fingers to her bedroom but made him sit in the corner. When she crept into her bed, he hopped over and reminded her of the promise she had made to let him sleep there also. But now the princess was so enraged that she picked him up and flung him into the furthest corner of the room. As the poor creature hit the wall he disappeared and a handsome young prince stood in his place.

He explained that many years ago a witch had placed a curse upon him and changed him into a frog. 'Only a young and beautiful princess had the power to break the spell.'

The young prince and princess soon became dear companions, and later got married and lived happily ever after.

The Old Woman Who Lived in a Vinegar Bottle

There was once an old woman who lived in a vinegar bottle. One day a kind fairy happened to be passing by and she heard a voice moaning:

'What a shame, what a shame. Why do I have to live in a vinegar bottle when a little cottage with a pretty garden would be so much better?'

The kind fairy took pity on the old lady and told her to close her eyes and turn around three times. This the old lady did and found herself in the loveliest cottage with a small but pretty rose garden surrounding it.

Many months passed and the kind fairy came by the little cottage and heard a grumbling voice saying:

'What a shame, what a shame. Why do I have to live in a pokey little cottage when a big mansion would be nicer?'

The fairy was surprised to hear these words but again took pity on the old woman, bade her close her eyes and turn around three times. When this was done, a mansion with wide sweeping lawns had replaced the cottage. Happy with her good deed, the fairy flew away to look for other people to help. It was many months before she was back that way but, lo and behold, what should she hear but a whining voice saying:

'What a shame, what a shame. Why should I have to suffer a draughty mansion like this when a royal palace and servants would make me far more comfortable? I want to be a queen and rule over the people.'

The fairy was angry to hear this but once again told the old woman to close her eyes and turn around three times. When she had done this the old woman had a crown on her head, wore splendid clothes and had a magnificent palace as her home, from which to rule over all the land and the people.

Many months later the fairy stopped by to visit the old woman but she flew into a rage when she heard the complaining voice again:

'What a shame, what a shame. Why should I have to live in such a small palace and rule over such a small country when I could rule over the whole world?'

So once again the kind fairy bade the woman turn around three times. This the old crone did but when she opened her eyes she found herself back in the vinegar bottle. The kind fairy didn't visit the old lady ever again.

Text Type: Myths	Term: Weeks:

Purpose	• To allow children the opportunity to experiment/approximate the genre of myths as they re-create the text • To allow children the opportunity to contemplate the use of myths to explain natural phenomena. • To provide children with a focus and a forum to discuss and explore techniques used in writing myths.

Immersion	Children should be provided with many opportunities to hear and read good examples of myths. Over several days the teacher should read a wide selection and each reading session should be followed by discussion. Children should be encouraged to read and re-read collections of myths at school and at home, and to share their favourites.

Retelling	Using the standard procedure, retelling of the following texts occurs over a two-week period: • Why the Kangaroo Hops • How Koalas Got Their Ears • How the Tiger Got Its Stripes

Responding

1. Teacher-initiated discussion — in either small group or whole class — of the question 'What makes a myth a myth?'.

2. Criteria should be displayed on a chart and compared with those of an authoritative publication such as an encyclopaedia.

3. These criteria may also be compared with those of fable and fairy tale.

4. Encourage children to use this knowledge as a basis for their own story writing.

Why the Kangaroo Hops

Nugget Jabangadi James

Long, long ago, in the Dreamtime, the kangaroo walked on his four legs like other animals. He did not hop as he does today, but he could run very fast.

Kangaroo was a shy animal and lived by himself. All day he woud lie in the shade of the mulga trees and at night he would go out on to the plains to eat grass.

One day while he was sleeping under the mulga trees, a bushfire blazed across the plains. Kangaroo woke up and tried to run to safety but he was caught by the flames.

As he ran through the fire his front paws were badly burnt. They were now much smaller, and burnt black. He could no longer run and was trapped in the middle of a fierce circle of fire.

Kangaroo was frightened and knew he was in great danger.

He decided he would have to run using only his strong back legs and his long tail. And so he hopped. He hopped as far as he could until he was very close to the fire.

Then he made a mighty leap over the top of the flames.

Kangaroo continued hopping until he was safe. When he tried to walk again on all four legs he found he couldn't, so he began hopping again and has done so ever since.

And if you look at a kangaroo's paws you will see where they were burnt black by the fire long, long ago.

How Koalas Got Their Ears

Karen-Anne Schier (5th grade)

Koalas long, long ago didn't have ears. They were just brown, cuddly and very plain. One koala named Jeroba was always comparing himself with other animals and, every time he did, he realised that all the other animals had ears and he didn't. This depressed him a great deal.

One day when he was walking along the cliff edge he met up with his friend Cloey the possum. As they were walking along, a squawking sound came from the bottom of the cliff. Jeroba was very curious and he wanted to know what it was. So he leaned forward a little bit. At that moment a bird flew above them yelping. Jeroba looked up and started to pull faces at the bird. Suddenly he lost his balance and he slipped off the edge of the cliff. Luckily Cloey had time to grab two large pinches of the brown furry skin on Jeroba's head.

Instead of him coming back up onto the cliff edge again, the skin stretched. Jeroba hung from Cloey's hands for over half an hour and by the time he was safe on the top of the cliff again he had two large flappy things on each side of his head. Jeroba called these ears. That's why nowadays koalas have ears.

How the Tiger Got Its Stripes

Le-Minh Hinh (5th grade)

In the jungles of India lived a family of tigers. One hot day baby tiger decided to go for a walk. Baby tiger walked for a long time and eventually came to an open grassy area that was being used as a camp site. A man sat in the sun painting his jeep with black paint. Baby tiger lay in the cool of the shade and watched. When the man had finished, he hung his wet paint brush on a low branch and went back to his tent.

Suddenly a small mouse jumped out of the bushes. The baby tiger saw this and thought it would be such good fun to catch the mouse. He pounced, but the mouse was much quicker and scampered through the trees out of reach. The baby tiger chased after him, under the dripping paint brush, and as he ran the black paint ran down his sides and the hot Indian sun dried it into wide stripes. That is how the tiger got its stripes.

Author Craft

The power of description to develop atmosphere, character and setting

Text Type: Author Craft— Atmosphere	Term: Weeks:

Purpose	<ul><li>To develop an awareness of the techniques used by authors to create a sense of mood/atmosphere in writing.</li><li>To allow children the opportunity to experiment/approximate these techniques as they re-create the text.</li><li>To allow children a focus and forum within which they can discuss author techniques.</li></ul>

Immersion	Children need many opportunities to hear and read examples of emotive writing. Texts which are useful to develop awareness are: *Charlotte's Web*, E. B. White — loneliness (Ch 4) *Lord of the Rings*, J. R. R Tolkien — fear/apprehension (Ch 12) *My Family and other Animals*, G. Durrell — homeliness (Ch 2) *The Lion, the Witch, and the Wardrobe*, C. S. Lewis — misery, fear, hope (Ch 11) *Alice in Wonderland*, L. Carroll — confusion Discussion/sharing of the feelings evoked, the images, leading into 'What is atmosphere?' and 'How was it created?'

Retelling	Using the standard procedure (but with emphasis on prediction and the concluding sharing sessions, to discuss the creation of atmosphere), retelling of the following texts occurs over a two-week period: • The Old Grey House • Death Alley • The Miserable Day

Responding	1. Children should be encouraged to write their own stories, or introduction to a story, incorporating a sense of mood/emotion.
	2. Encourage children to be aware of atmosphere/feelings when they read their own books.
	3. A collection of texts strong in emotion/atmosphere may be collated as a useful reference and resource for the classroom.

The Old Grey House

I was lost, cold and very frightened. The thunder cracked and roared and filled my ears and electric blue lightning lit up the bleak sky.

Then an old grey house loomed through the darkness, mist swirling around its doors and its dirty cracked windows. I had no option but to seek shelter from the storm.

Nervously I rang the rusty bell and heard it echo through every room, but no one answered. I called 'Hello, is anyone there?' but no one answered. Only an owl far away hooted twice in reply and then stopped.

Plucking up courage I pushed open the door and tiptoed into the house, which had no furniture, just a photo of an old woman smiling mysteriously. I sat down on the cold, carpetless floor and huddled with my knees near my chest for warmth.

Without warning, the hair on my neck prickled and an uncontrollable shiver shook my body. I felt as though there was someone else in the room, though I could hear no one and see no one. I looked at the photo on the wall and the eyes looked back at me, cold grey eyes that held no kindness. I knew I could not stay in this house any longer. It spelt danger. I ran across the room and out of the house, away from the danger and into the storm.

Death Alley

Neill Paxton (5th grade)

It was a cold harsh night and the wind was strong, blowing furiously through the never-ending alleys. It tossed up leaves and litter and turned them over with the least bit of care. This cycle took place time after time. Suddenly silence broke and there was a clash of garbage tins. A shadow covered the alley and a figure stumbled into sight. He huddled up into a corner of the alley. Slowly he raised the syringe into the air and gazed at it. With the most delicate touch the needle pierced the skin and drugs soon filled his body. As the street lights flickered he struggled to his feet. He followed the wall that was marked with graffiti. The night was long and the night was cold but the man fought for his life. Death was close and the rain pelted down on the garbage tins. The man crawled across the alley and paused for a while. The rain stopped and the man slowly stopped breathing.

The Miserable Day

Karen-Anne Schier (5th grade)

The rest of the afternoon was miserable, rain sprinkled down on roofs, smog and mist crept through streets and a strong wind howled around the houses. Old carts were wheeled through the town and the sound of horses being whipped was close. People hurried through alleyways under umbrellas and coats. Fishermen in raincoats and hats hurried about the boats, for they had just arrived from the last journey. A peasant girl walked along the sidewalk with not a single penny at hand. She paused to look at the fisherman hurry about the boats, throwing scales and fishheads overboard. She was very lonely so she tried to talk to the fishermen, but even they wouldn't talk to her. No one had ever talked to her all through the life she had already lived. She walked away sighing, the rain thumping against her back and her cold little feet sloshing in puddles.

Text Type: Author Craft— Character	Term: Weeks:

Purpose	• To develop an awareness of the descriptive technique used to create a clear picture of a character. • To allow children the opportunity to experiment with this technique as they re-create the text. • To allow children a focus and forum within which they can discuss author techniques.

Immersion	Children must be provided with many opportunities to hear and read texts which include good descriptions of, and development of, character. Texts which are useful in providing such good models are: *My Family and Other Animals*, G. Durrell — The Rose Beetle Man (Ch 3) *Danny, Champion of the World*, R. Dahl — Father (Chs 2 and 9) *The Hobbit*, J. R. R. Tolkien — Hobbits (Ch 1) *The Lion, the Witch, and the Wardrobe*, C. S. Lewis — Mr Tumnus (Chs 1 and 2) *Charlotte's Web*, E. B. White — Wilbur *Storm Boy*, C. Thiele — Fingerbone Bill

Retelling	Using the standard procedure (but with emphasis on prediction and the concluding sharing session, to discuss the descriptive technique of the author) retelling of the following texts occurs over a two-week period: • A Picture of My Father • Anne's Surprise • Long John Silver

Responding

1. Children should be encouraged to write their own character descriptions.

2. Encourage children to be aware of vivid character description and character development when they read their own books.

3. A collection of good character descriptions may be made and used as a classroom resource and reference.

4. Children should be encouraged to be aware of other indicators of character, e.g. how other people in the story react to the character.

A Picture of My Father
Roald Dahl

My father, without the slightest doubt, was the most marvellous and exciting father any boy ever had.

You might think, if you didn't know him well, that he was a stern and serious man. He wasn't. He was actually a wildly funny person. What made him appear so serious was the fact that he never smiled with his mouth. He did it all with his eyes. He had brilliant blue eyes and, when he thought of something funny, his eyes would flash and if you looked carefully, you could actually see a tiny little golden spark dancing in the middle of each eye. But the mouth never moved.

I am glad my father was an eye-smiler. It meant he never gave me a fake smile because it's impossible to make your eyes twinkle if you aren't feeling twinkly yourself. A mouth-smile is different. You can fake a mouth-smile any time you want, simply by moving your lips. I've also learned that a real mouth-smile always has an eye-smile to go with it, so watch out, I say, when someone smiles at you with his mouth but the eyes stay the same. It's sure to be bogus.

My father was not what you would call an educated man and I doubt if he had read twenty books in his life. But he was a marvellous story-teller. He used to make up a bedtime story for me every single night, and the best ones were turned into serials and went on for many nights running.

From *Danny the Champion of the World*

Anne's Surprise

Leanne McNiven (5th grade)

Anne was a small girl about the age of three but she was a very clever little girl all the same. She had black hair in a sort of bob cut and wherever she went, she wore a little red rose that Granny had given her. It wasn't real, of course, but that didn't matter. She loved going to visit Granny (she was an only child so she didn't ever have anyone to play with). Granny had a big box full of a lot of exciting things for little girls to play with. Whenever Anne went to visit Granny she would quietly go upstairs to the attic by herself and put on a big hat with a giant feather and a floppy dress covered with gold sequins. She would imagine that she was a posh lady walking down Avenue Street. Anne had a big imagination for such a tiny person. Sometimes she would pretend she was a tiny creature that moved so quietly no one could hear her. She could amuse herself very well that way. Anne's mother and father were very proud of their little girl.

Long John Silver

R. L. Stevenson

I remember him as if it were yesterday, as he
came plodding to the inn door, his sea-chest
following behind him in a hand-barrow; a tall,
strong, heavy, nut-brown man; his tarry pigtail
falling over the shoulders of his soiled blue coat;
his hands ragged and scarred, with black, broken
nails; and the sabre cut across one cheek, a dirty,
livid white. I remember him looking round the cove
and whistling to himself as he did so, and then
breaking out in that old sea-song that he sang so
often afterwards:

> 'Fifteen men on the dead man's chest—
> Yo-ho-ho, and a bottle of rum!'

in the high, old tottering voice that seemed to have
been tuned and broken at the capstan bars. Then
he rapped on the door with a bit of stick like a
handspike that he carried, and when my father
appeared, called roughly for a glass of rum. This,
when it was brought to him, he drank slowly, like a
connoisseur, lingering on the taste, and still looking
about him at the cliffs and up at our signboard.

from *Treasure Island*

Text Type: Author Craft— Setting	Term: Weeks:

Purpose	• To develop an awareness of the descriptive technique used to create a clear picture of the setting for a story.
	• To allow children the opportunity to experiment with this technique as they re-create the text.
	• To allow children a focus and forum within which they can discuss author techniques.

Immersion	Children must be provided with many opportunities to hear and read and react to texts which include good descriptions of setting. Texts which are useful in providing such good models are: *My Family and Other Animals*, G. Durrell—Daffodil Yellow Villa (Ch 7) *Lord of the Rings*, J. R. R. Tolkien—The Marshlands (Ch 11) *The Borrowers*, M. Norton—Arriety's room (Ch 2) *The Lion, the Witch and the Wardrobe*, C. S. Lewis—Narnia (Ch 1)—Witches' Castle (Chs 7, 9)

Retelling	Using the standard procedure (but with emphasis on prediction and the concluding sharing session to discuss the descriptive technique of the author) retelling of the following texts occurs over a two-week period: • The Barn • My Father's Garage • Aunt Gwen's House

Responding

1. Children should be encouraged to write their own description of a setting, maybe as the lead to a story.

2. Encourage children to be aware of clear descriptions of setting when they read their own books.

3. A collection of such good descriptions may be made and used in the classroom as a reference/resource.

4. In sharing sessions, encourage children to explore the relationships between setting/atmosphere/character development.

The Barn

E. B. White

The barn was very large. It was very old. It smelled
of hay and it smelled of manure. It smelled of the
perspiration of tired horses and the wonderful
sweet breath of patient cows. It often had a sort of
peaceful smell — as though nothing bad could
happen ever again in the world. It smelled of grain
and of harness dressing and of axle grease and of
rubber boots and of new rope. And whenever the
cat was given a fish-head to eat, the barn would
smell of fish. But mostly it smelled of hay, for there
was always hay in the great loft up overhead. And
there was always hay being pitched down to the
cows and the horses and the sheep.

The barn was pleasantly warm in winter when the
animals spent most of their time indoors, and it
was pleasantly cool in summer when the big doors
stood wide open to the breeze. The barn had stalls
on the main floor for the work horses, tie-ups on
the main floor for the cows, a sheepfold down
below for the sheep, a pigpen down below for
Wilbur, and it was full of all sorts of things that you
find in barns: ladders, grindstones, pitch forks,
monkey wrenches, scythes, lawn mowers, snow
shovels, axe handles, milk pails, water buckets,
empty grain sacks, and rusty rat traps. It was the
kind of barn that swallows like to build their nests
in. It was the kind of barn that children like to play
in. And the whole thing was owned by Fern's uncle,
Mr Homer L. Zuckerman.

from *Charlotte's Web*

My Father's Garage

When I was young my father owned a garage and every day after breakfast he would disappear into it and not emerge until my mother called him for lunch.

It was not a very large place but into it my father crowded spare parts and tools that hung from the walls and ceiling: fan belts and engines, exhaust pipes and tyres. The floor space was always occupied by a car needing repair.

It was a noisy place as my father hammered and tapped and as car engines raced back into life.

The garage smelt of oil and petrol and grease and so did my father. He was always banished to the bathroom before being allowed into the house after work.

The garage was such a part of my father's life that I cannot go into one now without being reminded of him.

Aunt Gwen's House

Philippa Pearce

. . . Aunt Gwen appeared in the doorway, laughing and wanting to kiss Tom. She drew him inside, and Uncle Alan followed with the luggage.

There were cold stone flags under Tom's feet, and in his nostrils a smell of old dust that it had been nobody's business to disperse. As he looked round, he felt a chill. The hall of the big house was not mean nor was it ugly, but it was unwelcoming. Here it lay at the heart of the house — for it went centrally from front to back with a sideways part to the stair-foot, in a T-shape — and the heart of the house was empty — cold — dead. Someone had pinned bright travel posters on to the high, grey walls: someone had left a laundry-box with its laundry-list, in a corner; there were empty milk-bottles against a far door, with a message to the milkman: none of these things seemed really to belong to the hall. It remained empty and silent — silent unless one counted the voice of Aunt Gwen chattering on about Tom's mother and Peter's measles. When her voice died for a moment, Tom heard the only sound that went on: the tick, and then tick, and then tick, of a grandfather clock.

from *Tom's Midnight Garden*

Text Type: Author Craft— Poetry	Term: Weeks:

Purpose	<ul><li>To develop an awareness of poetic expression, of vivid and intense imagery.</li><li>To allow children to explore such expression through the re-creation of text.</li><li>To allow children a focus and forum within which they can further discuss and explore poetry writing.</li></ul>
Immersion	Children must be provided with plenty of opportunities to hear, read and react to poetry. They must be allowed and encouraged to play around with the words. Lots of poetry should be read aloud and shared. Discussion should focus on the differences between poetry and prose but children must be allowed their opinions/ preferences. Lots of word play— alliteration, assonance, onomatopaeia, similes, metaphors— opens up the mind to poetry.
Retelling	Using the standard procedure, retelling of the following texts occurs over a two-week period: • Fang • The Death of a Cat • The Sea Horse Sharing: Discussion should look at phrasing, sentence structure— How is it different from prose?

Responding

1. Children should be encouraged to write their own poetry, to create word pictures and to engage in further word play.

2. Children may be encouraged to start their own personal anthologies of favourite poems and to share these with others.

3. Encourage children to be aware of vivid images/word pictures in the novels they read and then to contemplate the relationships between such writing and poetry.

Fang
Robin Klein

How come every other kid in this street has a great pet
    and I'm stuck with Fang?
I didn't pick him out, he just followed me home one
    day and wouldn't leave.
How come every other cat in this street purrs?
Fang makes a noise like a nuclear-powered tank
    revving up for business.
He turns his nose up at milk and prefers lapping:
water from the gully trap,
seepage from the compost heap,
water that the spinach has been cooked in,
oil slicks from the car.
The only food he likes is what he pinches from the
    Great Dane next door.

He hasn't got nice hobbies like other cats, such as:
chasing balls of paper,
swatting gently at flies,
climbing trees,
playing with ping-pong balls.
His hobby is stalking cars along the freeway.
I must be the only kid in this street who goes to bed
    wearing a crash helmet.
(Another one of his hobbies is dive-bombing people
    in bed.)
Visitors stand at our front gate and call out nervously,
    'Is Fang in or out?'
(He thinks visitors are the same species as Mouse.)

How come I'm the only kid in this street who likes him?

The Death of a Cat

Anthony Thompson

I rose early
On the fourth day
Of his illness,
And went downstairs
To see if he was
All right.
He was not in the
House, and I rushed
Wildly round the
Garden calling his name.
I found him lying
Under a rhododendron
Bush.
His black fur
Wet, and matted
With the dew.
I knelt down beside him,
And he opened his
Mouth as if to
Miaow
But no sound came.
I picked him up
And he lay quietly
In my arms
As I carried him
Indoors.
Suddenly he gave
A quiet miaow
And I felt his body tense
And then lie still.
I laid his warm
Lifeless body on
The floor, and
Rubbed my fingers
Through his fur.
A warm tear
Dribbled down
My cheek and
Left a salt taste
On my lips.
I stood up, and
Walked quietly
Out of the room.

The Sea Horse

Gaston Pedroza (5th grade)

The sea-horse vibrates its way through the dark
blue velvet sea.
Its eyes shine like diamonds on royal cushions and
its bony body looks like it was plated with armour.
The curled tail looks like a fish hook and its pipe-
like mouth sucks up food like a vacuum cleaner.
Its gentle swaying body resembles a kite in the sky
and the back fin looks like a Japanese fan.
It goes to sleep with its tail curled around branches
of seaweed.

Expository Text

Factual texts which describe, instruct, persuade, inform and argue

Text Type: Expository Text (Exploration)	Term: Weeks:

Purpose	• To expose children to non-fiction texts which explain, describe and argue.
	• To allow children to explore the genres of non-fiction by re-creating a text and to use such vocabulary in both an oral and written form.
	• To provide children with a focus and forum to discuss the differences between genre and between fictional and non-fictional writing.

Immersion	Because of the need for correctness in terms of information, immersion before non-fiction retellings needs to be thorough. Vocabulary should be displayed and used orally so that concepts are developed and children build up confidence in a topic. Discussions might focus on the reasons for exploration, pioneers in other fields, maps and time-lines. Useful books to read and share are:
	Christopher Columbus, C. Ingram Judson, Follet
	Christopher Columbus, Nelson
	The Cruise of Mr Christopher Columbus, Sadyebeth and Anson Lowitz, Ashton
	The Travels of Marco Polo, Brett, Collins
	How Men discovered the World, H. R. Hecke, Kaye and Ward

Famous Explorers, Macdonald
In History Exploration, D. Smith and
D. Newton, Schofield and Sims
Children's Britannica, Vols. 5, 7, 13, 16
The Young Scientist Book of Spaceflight,
Usborne

Retelling	Retelling of non-fiction requires a great deal of concentration and therefore quiet; retelling is probably best conducted on a whole-class basis. Prediction can be in the form of brainstorming with the vocabulary written up and left displayed. This then frees children from having to juggle vocabulary, spelling, concepts and sentence structure, etc. Over two weeks texts to be retold: • Discovery of the Unknown East • Discovery of the Americas • Space: The New Frontier • Space Travel vs Famine Relief

Responding	1. Encourage further reading/sharing of information on exploration. 2. Discuss realities of reading/writing non-fiction.

Discovery of the Unknown East

Marco Polo was born of an adventurous father in Venice, Italy, in the year 1254. Throughout his childhood he did not see his father who had embarked on a long journey to China to the palace of Kubla Khan.

Travel in those days was a treacherous business: maps were scarce and few people could use them; bandits were everywhere and people had to travel overland by horse or on foot; sea travel was worse with poorly constructed ships that were often lost at sea.

In spite of this Marco, his father and uncle set off for China when the boy was only 15 years old.

During their travels, the adventurers saw many marvels: a fountain of oil which came out of the earth in Persia; exotic mosques and gardens in Baghdad; mirages in the great Gobi Desert.

In all, it took the explorers three years to reach the city of Peking in China. The Chinese Emperor Kubla Khan became very fond of Marco and made him governor of one of his cities. He governed fairly and became popular. Eventually, however, Kubla Khan became ill and the three Venetians decided that it was time for them to leave China and return to Italy.

The incredible journey overland and by sea made by these men was written down and became the inspiration for future explorers. Indeed, Columbus took a copy of this book with him many years later when he made his discovery of The West Indies.

Discovery of the Americas

Christopher Columbus was born in 1451 and died in 1506 at the age of 55. But in that short life he managed to discover a whole new world, although he did not know it at the time. This new world was the American continent.

The Queen of Spain was the person who made his tremendous discovery possible. When no other wealthy person would finance his expedition, she came to his aid. In 1492 she provided Columbus with three ships: the Pinta, the Nina and the Santa Maria. However, it is not the ships that make a good explorer. What Columbus had that no other sailor at the time had was a great sense of adventure. He believed that if he sailed westward from Europe, sooner or later he would come to India. He believed that this would be a less hazardous journey to India than sailing around Africa. Columbus and his tiny fleet set off from the shores of Spain and ten weeks later land was sighted. It was one of the islands now known as the Bahamas that lie just off the coast of Central America.

Columbus made four journeys altogether to America, each time discovering new places.

He was honoured by the Queen of Spain for his discoveries, but in later years, the people forgot what a brave explorer he had been and he died a lonely man.

Space: the New Frontier

One of the greatest feats of modern times has to be the expedition of people to the Moon. In July 1969 a spaceship launched Apollo 11 on its journey. It carried three very skilful astronauts — Aldrin, Armstrong and Collins.

The space flight and subsequent landing on the lunar surface went perfectly. Early on the morning of July 21 Neil Armstrong opened the hatch of the Lunar Module *Eagle* and slowly climbed down to the Moon's surface. Shortly afterwards he was joined by Edwin Aldrin. For $2^1/_2$ hours the two scientists collected samples of rock and dust and set up scientific equipment. They also planted an American flag to show that they had landed first. However, they could not claim the territory for the USA as early explorers might have done. These men were part of a new breed of explorers, who risked journeys into the unknown, not for riches or to conquer new lands, but to further our knowledge of the universe. Space is now the new frontier for exploration. Who knows how far we will travel in the future, in search of knowledge and adventure?

Space Travel vs Famine Relief

The front page headline read:

> '5 Billion Dollar Project—
> USA to search for life on Mars'

On page 4 of the same newspaper the headline read:

> 'Bob Geldorf Concert to raise money
> for Africa's starving millions.'

The controversy over whether money should be spent on space travel, when millions don't have enough to eat, has been going on for many years.

Supporters of space travel have many arguments:

1. People need to find another planet upon which humans could exist should there ever be a need to evacuate Earth.

2. Scientists need the information sent back from space travel to find out how the universe began.

3. Humans need to find resources of minerals on close planets because Earth's resources won't last forever.

All of these arguments are concerned with our future. However, there are people who say that this money would be best spent now and let the future take care of itself. Every year droughts and floods cause famine in many countries in Africa and South America. These countries are very poor and their governments cannot afford to provide food to keep their people alive until they can grow their own. So every year millions die and charities in wealthier countries try to raise money to help the starving. 'If only the money spent on such things as space travel could be donated,' they say, 'millions of people could be saved.'

The dispute will no doubt go on and on. Meanwhile, millions will continue to die while people push further into the depths of our universe.

Text Type: Expository Text (Mysteries)	Term: Weeks:

Purpose	<ul><li>To expose children to non-fiction texts which use sub-headings as text organisers, and maps which complement information.</li><li>To allow children to explore such texts by retelling in a written form.</li><li>To provide children with a focus and forum to discuss the assistance/necessity of sub-headings and maps to comprehension.</li></ul>

Immersion	Sub-headings and explanatory maps are a regular feature of expository writing, so the teacher must provide plenty of models of such texts to display and discuss. Useful texts are: *The World Atlas of Mysteries*, F. Hitching *Mysteries, Monsters and Untold Secrets*, G. Laycock *Mysterious Powers and Strange Forces*, Usborne *The Loch Ness Monster*, Macdonald *The Loch Ness Monster*, *Explore* Magazine (3)

Retelling	The retelling is probably best conducted on a whole-class basis. The prediction could take the form of brainstorming words with vocabulary written up and displayed throughout the retelling for reference by children. Texts to be retold over two weeks: • The Bermuda Triangle • Loch Ness Monster Sharing after retelling should pick up on the use of sub-headings as an aid to writing as well as to reading.

Responding

1. Children should be encouraged to share expository texts which use maps and sub-headings, explaining their purpose and aid to comprehension.

2. Children should be encouraged to use these aids in their own non-fiction writing, where appropriate.

The Bermuda Triangle

One of the most intriguing mysteries of the present times must surely be that of the Bermuda Triangle. This is an area of sea off the coast of Florida and the Bahamas.

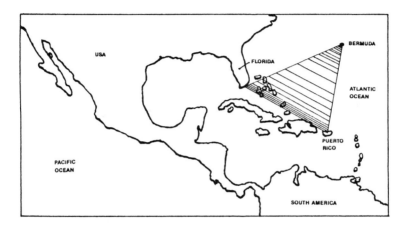

Ever since the 15th century, this area has been associated with weird happenings. When Columbus sailed through the Triangle on his discovery voyage, he reported that the sea glowed and a fire ball shot out of the ocean.

In more recent times, pilots have reported that when flying over the area all control of the plane was lost; others that the aeroplane glowed with green light. Since 1945 more than 100 planes and more than 1000 people have vanished in this area, leaving no hint of what might have happened.

None of these events can be easily explained. However, since ships and aircraft passing through the area nearly always report interference with compasses, scientists feel that it may be due to some strong magnetic force below the earth's surface.

Loch Ness Monster

Setting   In the mountainous country of Scotland there is a long and narrow lake called Loch Ness. It is a beautiful place surrounded by hills and glens covered in purple heather. However, the lake is very deep and rather dangerous.

Puzzle of Loch Ness   Loch Ness has for many years been considered a most mysterious place. There have been many reported sightings of a monster living in the lake. Some reports claimed that the creature was more than twelve metres long, with a scaly neck and horns on its head. Others said it had two humps like a camel and flippers like a seal. Whatever the reports, they have all told of a creature unlike any animal known on Earth today.

Research   Scientists and film makers have often tried to get more information and actual pictures of this creature (if it really does exist). But no one so far has found any real evidence. This has led many people to disbelieve the stories of the Loch Ness Monster and to suggest that what has been seen is really driftwood or something similar. However, not everyone is convinced of this and the mystery remains.

What do you think?

Text Type: Expository Text (Rainforests)	Term: Weeks:

Purpose	• To expose children to expository prose which explains and which persuades. • To enable children to see that information can be presented in a diagrammatic form. • To allow children to explore such texts by retelling in a written form. • To provide children with a focus and forum to discuss the value of, and implications of, such writing/texts.
Immersion	During teacher reading and sharing, part of the focus should be on vocabulary and how it differs from that used in fiction, on layout, headings, diagrams. Encourage children to share their own readings. Useful texts: *Rainforests*, F. Crome, Hodder and Stoughton *Rainforest*, A. Fairley, Methuen *The Rainforest*, S. Parker, Bay Books
Retelling	'Rainforests' and 'Preserve Our Rainforest' may be done (over two weeks) using the standard retelling procedure. Emphasis on the power of persuasion through writing should be discussed after the retelling. The diagram should be treated differently: while it is possible and profitable to get children to predict after telling them that it is a diagram, the actual retelling should be done with the diagram visible. During the discussion the purpose/usefulness of diagrams should be emphasized.

Responding   1. Children should be encouraged to talk about their reading of texts which use diagrams.

2. Children should be encouraged to present information in diagrammatic form in their own expository writing.

Rainforests

What is a rainforest?

A rainforest is another name for a jungle. It grows
in places which have plenty of rain, good soil and
protection from winds. The trees in rainforests are
large and grow so close together that very little
light can penetrate through the leaves. The dense
cover of foliage formed by the trees is called a
canopy. Because of this canopy, rainforests are
shady places which make it impossible for grass or
small flowering plants to grow. Instead, the ground
is covered by fallen leaves, rotting logs, masses of
ferns, moss and lichens. Ferns also grow on tree
trunks, fighting for space with lianas or jungle vines
which twist around each other and form loops and
swings.

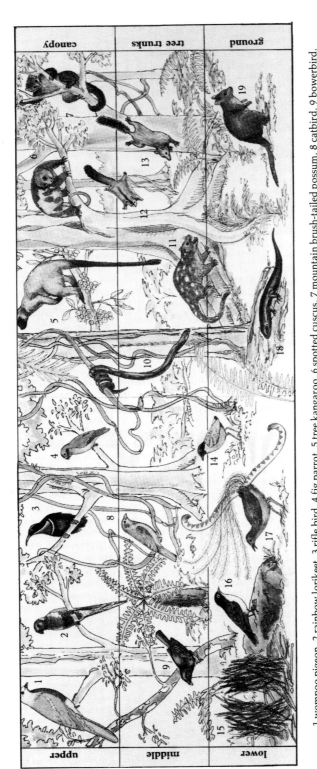

canopy — tree trunks — ground

upper — middle — lower

1 wompoo pigeon. 2 rainbow lorikeet. 3 rifle bird. 4 fig parrot. 5 tree kangaroo. 6 spotted cuscus. 7 mountain brush-tailed possum. 8 catbird. 9 bowerbird. 10 carpet snake. 11 tiger cat. 12 glider. 13 brush-tailed phascogale. 14 noisy pitta. 15 bower of satin bowerbird. 16 log runner. 17 lyrebird. 18 land mullet. 19 pademelon. (Not drawn to scale.)

Preserve Our Rainforest

Two hundred years ago Australia had large expanses of rainforest — lush areas of tall, densely packed trees — home to many unusual creatures.

However, the early settlers who followed Captain Cook cleared vast sections of this rainforest. They cleared land so that they could farm, run cattle and grow crops. But in doing this, they destroyed much of the rainforest. They also destroyed other sections of rainforest which they logged for the rich, red cedar trees which were wanted by furniture makers. And so our rainforest started to disappear — now there is not very much left.

Australia must realise that the rainforest which remains must be preserved; clearing for farming and logging for timber must stop now before all our rainforest is destroyed. Many animals need the rainforest to survive; the cuscus and tree kangaroo live only in rainforest areas. What will happen to them if we don't stop the destruction of our jungles? The government should preserve all rainforest as national parks so that all Australians, now and in the future, may enjoy their beauty.

Text Type: Expository Text (Read-do-retell)	Term: Weeks:

Purpose	• To familiarise children with the genre of instructional writing. • To allow children to explore this by a read-do-retell method. • To provide children with a focus and forum whereby they can discuss instructional writing, its precision and format and its difference from other non-fictional writing.

Immersion	Various forms of instructional reading should be provided for children to read and share and talk through. The particular features should be examined . . . lists of materials, methods of operation . . . recipe books, natural science activity cards, art and craft books, etc. provide good models.

Retelling	This activity is best done in small groups, maybe with selective assistance from volunteer parents. Tools and ingredients must be prepared beforehand and enough time allowed for a read-do-retell session. Children should be encouraged to read individually and then share their interpretations with the others in the group before starting the actual activity. Retelling of the text should be done soon after the practical activity. Sharing can later be done as a whole-class activity.

Responding	Children should be encouraged/permitted to do more read-do-retell activities from other available texts, such as natural science experiments, and to share with others the clarity or otherwise of those instructional texts.

Pikelets

Ingredients
1 egg
1 tablespoon sugar
1/2 cup milk
1 cup self-raising flour
2 teaspoons margarine
a little extra margarine

Tools
teaspoon
tablespoon
measuring cup
mixing spoon
mixing bowl
sieve
frypan
spatula

Method
1. Put the egg, sugar and 1/2 cup of milk into the mixing bowl. Beat well.
2. Sift the flour into the mixture and stir until it is mixed in completely.
3. Melt the margarine and stir into mixture.
4. Heat a little extra margarine in a frypan and drop spoonfuls of mixture in to cook.
5. When the pikelets bubble, turn them over and cook the other side.
6. Continue until they are all cooked.
7. Serve spread with butter or favourite topping.

Roller Pattern

Materials
plasticine
bottle or rolling pin
pencil
cotton reel
art paper
paint—2 or 3 colours
paintbrush
sharp stick

Directions
1. Using the bottle/rolling pin, roll out the plasticine until it is nice and flat and quite thin.
2. Push the pencil through the hole in the cotton reel so that it sticks out both ends.
3. Cut a strip of plasticine wide enough to wrap around the cotton reel.
4. With a sharp stick make patterns on the plasticine.
5. Paint the plasticine with a thin layer of paint and roll it across the paper.

This pattern will repeat itself over and over until the paint wears off. If you want to try another colour, wipe off the old paint first.

Text Type: Maps	Term: Weeks:

Purpose	• To expose children to information presented in map form.
	• To allow children to explore this method of presenting information and to use geographic terminology/vocabulary in an oral and written form.
	• To encourage children to categorise information when writing.

Immersion	Map reading should be preceded by lots of teacher modelling, using a large wall map and explaining geographic language (north east, mountain range, surrounding bodies of water, equator, etc.) Children should then be encouraged to choose a map and talk about it. Encourage the use of geographic indicators/vocabulary and stress the importance of being specific, categorising information and drawing inferences, e.g. 'Because Rockhampton lies on the Tropic of Capricorn I think the climate would be . . .'

Retelling	This retelling should use an open-book format and may be done using photocopied sheets or by working directly from an atlas. During sharing, ask the children to listen carefully to how the information is presented and the use of vocabulary.

Responding

1. Give the children a map outline with no detail and also a written retelling of the same map. From the information given, the children should try to reconstruct the map.

2. Discuss whether the information given was specific enough or whether more precise indicators such as degrees of latitude/longitude needed to be stated.

South America

33

CARIBBEAN SEA

Windward Islands

HONDURAS
Tegucigalpa
NICARAGUA
Managua
San Jose
COSTA RICA
PANAMA
Panama
Medellin
Cali
COLOMBIA
Bogota
Quito
ECUADOR

Maracaibo
Caracas
Trinidad and Tebago
Port of Spain
VENEZUELA
GUYANA
Georgetown
Paramaribo
SURINAM
Cayenne
FRENCH GUIANA
GUIANA HIGHLANDS

ATLANTIC OCEAN

Lima
Arequipa
Antofagasta
Santiago
Juan Fernandez Islands
Concepcion

Ancohuma
6550
La Paz
BOLIVIA
Sucre
PARAGUAY
Asuncion
Aconcagua
6960
Cordoba
ARGENTINA
URUGUAY
Montevideo
Buenos Aires
Bahia Blanca

Manaus
Belem
Teresina
Fortaleza
Recife
Salvador
Brasilia
BRAZILIAN HIGHLANDS
Belo Horizonte
Rio de Janeiro
Sao Paulo
Porto Alegre

B R A Z I L

PACIFIC OCEAN

ATLANTIC OCEAN

Falkland Islands

Tierra del Fuego
Cape Horn

6000
4000
2000
500
Sea Level
METRES

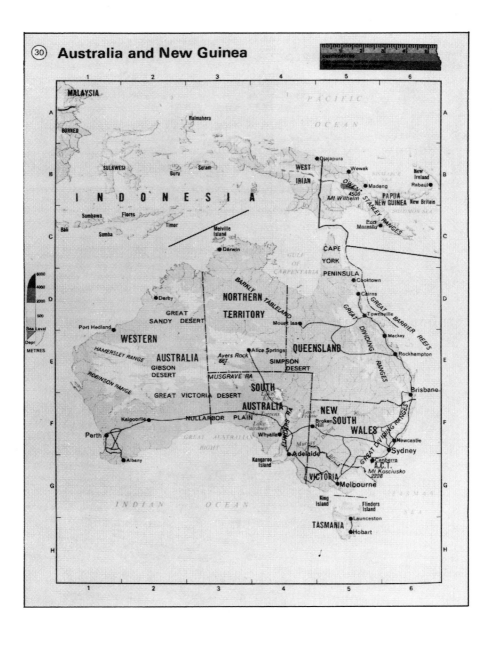

MALAYSIA

BORNEO

Halmahera

SULAWESI Buru Seram

I N D O N E S I A

Sumbawa Flores

Bali

Sumba Timor

Melville Island

Darwin

Djajapura

Wewak

WEST IRIAN

OWEN Madang New Ireland

Mt. Wilhelm 4508 PAPUA Rabaul

NEW GUINEA New Britain

SOLOMON SEA

Port Moresby

PACIFIC

OCEAN

CAPE YORK PENINSULA

GULF OF CARPENTARIA

Cooktown

Cairns

GREAT BARRIER REEFS

Townsville

Derby

GREAT SANDY DESERT

NORTHERN TERRITORY

BARKLY TABLELAND

Mount Isa

GREAT DIVIDING RANGES

Mackay

Port Hedland

WESTERN AUSTRALIA

HAMERSLEY RANGE GIBSON DESERT

Ayers Rock 867

Alice Springs

SIMPSON DESERT

QUEENSLAND

Rockhampton

ROBINSON RANGE

MUSGRAVE RA

SOUTH AUSTRALIA

Brisbane

GREAT VICTORIA DESERT

Kalgoorlie

NULLARBOR PLAIN

Lake Torrens

Lake Frome

NEW SOUTH WALES

Perth

GREAT AUSTRALIAN BIGHT

Lake Gairdner

Broken Hill

Whyalla

Murray

Newcastle

Sydney

Albany

Kangaroo Island

Adelaide

Canberra A.C.T.

Mt Kosciusko 2228

VICTORIA

Melbourne

INDIAN OCEAN

King Island

Flinders Island

TASMAN SEA

TASMANIA

Launceston

Hobart

8000 4000 2000 500 Sea Level Depr METRES

Centimetres

Text Type: Diagrams	Term: Weeks:

Purpose	• To expose children to flow diagrams. • To make children aware that information need not always be presented as a text. • To help children learn to write in a report form. • To encourage children to categorise information when writing.

Immersion	1. *Cloud types* — reading/discussion of the various cloud types, their appearance and significance — daily observation will confirm and clarify. 2. Experiments to illustrate concepts of evaporation, condensation, precipitation. (Useful reference: *A Teacher's Guide to Practical Science in the Primary School* (Sale)) 3. Expose children to a range of flowcharts, e.g. food chains, and to the concept of metamorphosis — look at the life cycles of frog, butterfly, cicada, bird, humans.

Retelling	Open-book retelling with instructions to tell it to someone who has not seen the diagram. Stress the need to be specific and comprehensive. During discussion, ask children to listen carefully to how the information is presented and to the use of vocabulary.

Responding   1. Encourage children to read other flowcharts and share with others.

2. Written retellings of a flowchart could be used and children asked to reconstruct the flow diagram from the text.

THE WATER CYCLE

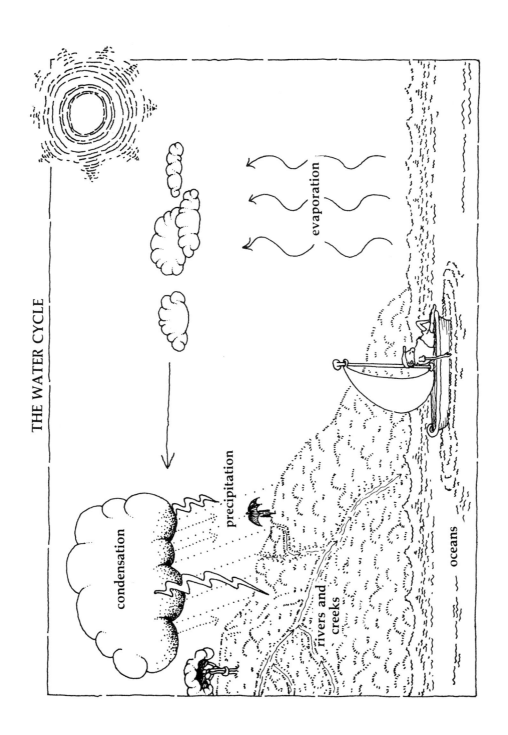

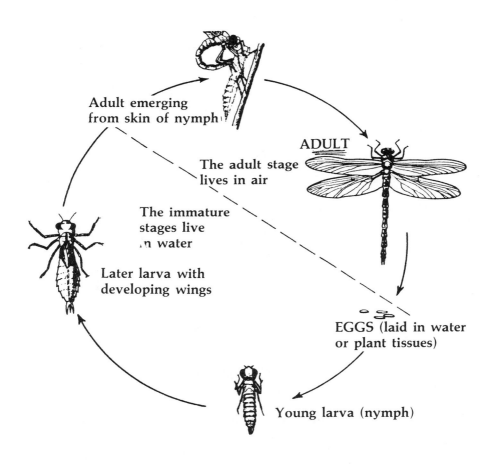

Adult emerging
from skin of nymph

ADULT

The adult stage
lives in air

The immature
stages live
in water

Later larva with
developing wings

EGGS (laid in water
or plant tissues)

Young larva (nymph)

Life story of a dragonfly showing incomplete change in appearance
as it grows to adulthood

Text Type: Charts	Term: Weeks:

Purpose	• To make children aware that information need not always be presented as continuous text. • To expose children to information presented in chart form. • To help children learn to write in a report form. • To provide children with a focus and forum to share and discuss information presented in charts.

Immersion	There are many and varied charts in schools from which teachers can provide excellent demonstrations. Attention should be drawn both to the information found in illustrations/diagrams and to that presented as text. Useful preparation for the following retellings is Methuen's *The Prehistoric Giants* (Poster Book).

Retelling	Open-book retelling with instructions to tell it to someone who has not seen the chart. Stress the need to be precise, to categorise information and to try to supplement facts with inferences drawn from the illustration, e.g. 'The Barosaurus had a long neck like a giraffe. It probably fed on trees like giraffes do.' The sharing session is an excellent time to discuss the differences between facts and inferences.

Responding

1. Encourage children to do more retellings from charts whenever it applies in other subject areas.

2. Get the children in groups to construct lists of the kind of information which would be essential to accompany charts — animals, countries, machines, etc. E.g., a chart on *countries* should include the country's name, location, temperature range, rainfall, population, major cities, important landforms, etc.

Torosaurus

'tor-o-saw-rus'	**Size** 7 metres long	**Facts** ● its neck frill may have supported huge cheek muscles
Name means 'bull lizard'	**Fossils** found in North America	
Food plants	**Date** late Cretaceous	

Barosaurus

'bar-o-saw-rus'	Size up to 27 metres long	Facts ● had weak teeth shaped like pencils ● had hollow bones
Name means 'heavy lizard'	**Fossils** found in Africa, North America	
Food plants	**Date** late Jurassic	

5

The Retelling Procedure and the Evaluation of Literacy Development

In the first chapter we made this statement:

'As well as noting these kinds of growth in our pupils, we also found that the retelling procedure helped the teacher with the task of evaluating and assessing literacy growth. The written retellings which learners produced (what we called their 'retelling texts'), and their behaviour while they produced them, became valuable sources of information about literacy development. We found that if we sampled our learners' written retellings over time, and used these in conjunction with other information, we could make evaluative statements about their:

- reading ability
- control of various genre
- control of many aspects of the writing process
- control of the conventions of written language.

We considered this to be an extra benefit of the retelling procedure because we had been struggling with the problems of evaluation/ assessment in literacy development for some time. Here, in a nutshell, was the kind of problem we'd been trying to deal with.

The Problems of Evaluating Literacy Development

Like many other teachers in the past, we'd been uneasy about the task of monitoring, evaluating and assessing literacy development. This uneasiness was exacerbated by the shift we made from a fragmented, behaviouristic view of language learning to a wholistic/natural learning approach. The principles which underpinned the wholistic/natural learning approach necessitated a new way of approaching the act of teaching. We realised later that a completely new pedagogy was emerging, different from anything we'd been conscious of before.

It became obvious that a different view of assessment, and a different set of assessment strategies, would be required. We realised that whatever form of assessment we eventually developed, it would have to be an approach which drew mainly on the methods of qualitative data collection: careful observation of individuals over time, especially as they engaged in literacy-related processes; interview procedures; and analysis of the various products ('artefacts') which resulted from their engagement in literacy-related activities.

When we looked closely at the traditional approaches to assessment which we'd been trying to use, it became obvious that they were based on quite different assumptions from those which underpin this new approach to learning language. For example, traditional forms of assessment involving such things as reading ages and numerical grades assume that various forms of language behaviour (i.e. reading, writing, spelling, talking, phonic ability) are separate, independent domains of knowledge and/or expertise, and that a score on some kind of test or checklist represents an immutable, unchanging degree of learning or knowledge or skill that the learner has reached.

When we became careful observers of learners' behaviours we quickly discovered that, when one looks at language wholistically, such things as 'knowledge' and 'degrees of learning' can change from occasion to occasion, and even during the same occasion. In other words, development in literacy is not linear. It is recursive. As Kemp states: '. . . in a wholistic literacy curriculum . . . assessment is that much more difficult because it is **change** that is being measured, not **stability**, and this requires that the teacher must be eternally vigilant' (Kemp 1986, p219, emphasis added).

How Do You Maintain Such 'Eternal Vigilance'?

We believe the answer to this is quite straightforward: Teachers must continually build up a store of knowledge about each learner's literacy development.

In order to do this, teachers need to learn some of the skills of the classical anthropologist. Anthropologists alternate between participant-observers, detached observers and collectors of artefacts. At times, they observe the 'members of the tribe' from a distance, recording their observations for later analysis. At other times, they ask questions of various informants about what they think and the ways they produce their artefacts, all the time recording their responses. These records become their stores of knowledge, from which they try to reconstruct what 'reality' is for the tribe or culture which is being observed.

In the case of a teacher, building up a store of knowledge about literacy development is the reality she is trying to construct. The reality is how each one of her pupils is changing and developing over time in their degrees of knowledge and skill in literacy, and all that literacy entails.

What Kind of Knowledge Do You Collect?

The answer to this question depends on the aims and objectives which have been set. Given the aims and objectives we established to guide our literacy program (Chapter 1), we decided we wanted to 'build up a store of knowledge' about each child in the class from two kinds of data:

1. Data which permitted us to draw conclusions about each learner's attitudes toward literacy and literacy learning. If one of our aims was to produce learners who would continue to use reading and writing outside the classroom, a necessary prerequisite was that they should feel positive about themselves as readers and writers (and talkers and thinkers), and positive about the continued use of reading, writing and other forms of language.

2. Data which permitted us to draw conclusions about each learner's developing control of the processes which underpin effective language use, especially those related to effective text construction, using both reading and writing as well as oral forms of language. Effective language use, in all its manifestations, depends upon knowing about, and doing things with, language. In order to read effectively, one must operate on texts in a certain way. One must bring into play certain processes. In order to write effectively, one must draw on strategies from a repertoire of certain processes, and use them together with certain knowledge about written texts and how they can be used.

What has this to do with the retelling procedure?

We found that the retelling procedure provided us with a unique opportunity to tap into both these kinds of data (attitude and knowledge) in ways which didn't violate the principles on which a wholistic/natural learning view of language is based. Over time, the store of knowledge which we built up on each child's literacy development gave us a very rich and detailed picture of the changes which were taking place. We also found that instead of waiting for something to happen so that we could record it, we could 'contrive' the situation, to a certain degree so that specific information about development in specific areas of literacy could be revealed.

In what follows, we illustrate and explain how one teacher used the retelling procedure to build up a store of knowledge which she then used to complement other data she'd been collecting as she worked with the children each day. The data collected during retelling sessions was used in conjunction with other data gathered in the busy ebb and flow of the classroom interactions typical of whole-language/natural learning classrooms. All this information becomes helpful when trying to assess what the children in such classrooms know and feel about literacy.

A Note of Caution

We have a number of concerns about the retelling procedure and its role in evaluation/assessment in a whole-language/natural learning classroom.

There is the possibility of misusing and/or distorting the original intent of the retelling procedure. Our concerns are:

1. If teachers set out to use the retelling procedure solely (or mainly) as an evaluative procedure, then it will be minimally useful as a whole-language teaching activity. The retelling procedure, as we designed it, should be used as part of an ongoing system which fosters language development. It should be seen as an opportunity to **use language to learn about language.** In other words, what teachers observe during retelling sessions is just one source of possible data about language development. Retelling sessions should be seen as one of the many language events which can provide input into the overall picture of language development which is being built up each day through careful observation of ongoing language behaviours. What is gleaned as a consequence of using retelling sessions will either confirm what has been observed in other contexts, or it will provide new insights into the degrees of language control which learners are developing (or not developing).

2. The store of knowledge built up by careful observation of the retelling procedure should therefore be used only to complement the evaluation process in any classroom. We don't believe there is any one ideal way to use the retelling procedure as a means of evaluation. The kinds of information which are built up from using retelling sessions to tap into language growth will change as teachers become more knowledgeable about language and language learning. The process of evaluation as we perceive it has been described by our colleague Jan Turbill.

Evaluation in language is a process of collecting a range of information, preferably in the everyday ebb-and-flow of classroom activity. It should be information which can be fine-tuned and paraphrased to suit the needs of the different 'stakeholders' in the child's literacy development. Turbill has identified a range of possible stakeholders who at various times, and for various reasons, will need to be informed of different learners' literacy development. In this range she includes the learners themselves, the teacher

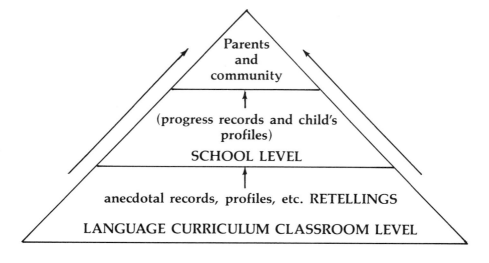

herself, the principal and other teachers, parents, the broader community. Depending on the purpose and the content there could well be others. Although the form in which the evaluation information might be presented will be different for each stakeholding audience, it emerges from the same source — the ongoing observation of learners as they attempt to learn language, learn through language, and learn about language, in the classroom. Turbill represents this schematically as shown on page 115.

We believe that the retelling procedure, as we describe it in this book, is one variety of data-collection which can be used. It fits into the bottom third of the 'evaluation triangle' presented above.

In what follows, we demonstrate how one teacher, with no specialist knowledge of linguistics or rhetoric, used the data which she collected from the retelling procedure to help her evaluate and assess what the language learners in her class were achieving.

THE RETELLING PROCEDURE: A TIME-LINE OF TEACHING/LEARNING ACTIVITIES

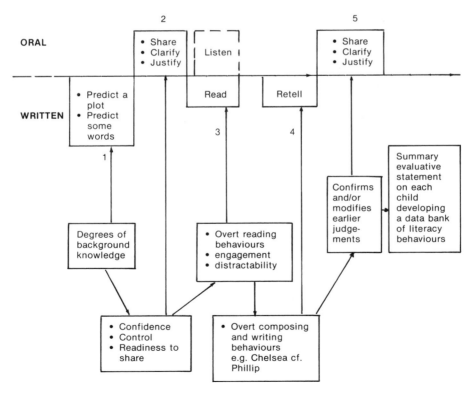

On-going opportunities to evaluate

A Case Study of Assessment/Evaluation Procedures Using the Retelling Procedure

The retelling procedure provides a number of different opportunities for teachers to form what we call **'evaluative opinions'** about what they consider to be important indicators of literacy development. These evaluative opinions build up into substantive pictures of development and become the basis for evaluative judgments. We can plot these opportunities to gather data along this time-line of steps in the retelling session.

Background to the Retelling Session

The case study will use the same retelling session described in Chapter 3, that is, the persuasive, argumentative text entitled 'Preserve our Rainforests'. You will recall that this was the third retelling session to be attempted in the theme entitled 'Rainforests'. The children were aged between 10 and 11 years and in Grade 5.

During the immersion phase of the theme (i.e. the previous two weeks), the teacher had conducted shared-book lessons using rainforest texts, providing the children with some to read during SSR time, talking herself, and encouraging the children to discuss what they'd been reading and hearing about rainforests.

Predict a Plot, Predict Some Words: Evaluation/Assessment Opportunity I

The first opportunity to begin to form tentative evaluative opinions about the participants occurs in the first two predicting phases of the session. Here are the responses which each child in the group made to this part of the lesson:

Chelsea: 'I think it will be about people who want to keep the rainforests of Australia.'

Leanne: '. . . about saveing (sic) a rainforest and why we should.'

Phillip: '. . . about people looking at a rainforest.'

Branco: '. . . maybe about how rainforest (sic) have changed since olden days.'

Le-Minh: '. . . about someone who going (sic) to tell you about a rainforest.'

By observing carefully what each member of the group predicts, the teacher can begin to form evaluative opinions about how successful the previous two weeks' immersion has been, and about the kind/extent of background knowledge which each child is bringing to the retelling session. For example, some evaluative opinions which the teacher formed on the basis of these responses were:

1. Chelsea and Leanne both understand the meaning of the word 'preserve' and obviously have a good deal of background knowledge of rainforests

and the conservation issues associated with them. They are also possibly aware that it is not a simple narrative piece. Their predictions give a slight hint that they realise this piece will be of an expository kind. Leanne's spelling of 'saveing' could be of possible interest when considering her control of surface features of text.

2. Le-Minh, Branco and Phillip possibly don't understand the meaning of 'preserve' and possibly are not too sure whether it will be a narrative or piece of exposition. The errors of syntax (inflection, auxiliary) signal a possible NESB-based problem for Branco and Le-Minh.

When these observations are considered with what we know about the background contexts each child comes from, they are consistent. On a previous occasion the teacher had noted the following about each child:

1. Chelsea and Leanne are from families which try to provide plenty of firsthand experiences of such things as rainforest for their children.

2. Le-Minh and Branco are NESB children. Parents are caring and work hard to provide material things for their children.

3. Phillip's family pursues competitive sport.

When the children were asked to predict some words which they might expect to encounter in a text with the plot they had predicted, they made these responses.

Chelsea: 'save, conditions, rainforest'
Leanne: 'save, children, rainforest'
Phillip: (Phillip made no predictions at the word level)
Branco: '300, 200, etc, years ago, vines, canopy, moisture'
Le-Minh: 'rainforest, cutting, die, save'

The evaluative opinions formed by the teacher from these data were:

1. Chelsea and Leanne have predicted words which conform clearly to their predictions.

2. Le-Minh's predicted words suggest that she does know what preserve means, and possibly knows more than her predict-a-plot indicates. This probably has something to do with a lack of control over English. When predicting a plot she had to operate at the sentence level. When predicting words she only has to operate at the word level. Perhaps this suggests that Le-Minh's ability to operate at the word level is more under control than her ability to operate at the sentence level?

3. Phillip appears to be confused by the title and doesn't have the confidence to pursue it any further. Perhaps when Phillip gets the chance to share and hear other people's interpretations he will get a clearer picture?

4. Branco is displaying obvious knowledge about rainforests, but is not too sure about the interpretation of the title.

Sharing after Prediction: Evaluation/Assessment Opportunity II

In the ideal retelling classroom, sharing is voluntary. Allowing for this permits confidence to develop and confidence is an indirect index of control. Confidence in sharing is an indicator of control of process, and of control of information. Here is a summary from videotape records, of what transpired in sharing time in this lesson.

Teacher: 'It's now time to share our predictions.'

Chelsea, without being asked or called upon, responds. She reads her plot prediction and her words.

Chelsea: 'I think it will be about people who want to keep the rainforests of Australia. Save, conditions, rainforest.'

Teacher: 'Why do you say that?'

Chelsea: 'Because preserve means save and on the TV I heard them about trying to stop the logging of rainforest in Tasmania.'

Teacher: 'Anyone like to make a comment on Chelsea's predictions?'

Leanne agrees with Chelsea's predictions. She offers similar reasons demonstrating a knowledge of the word 'preserve'. Her family experiences provided the basis for her knowledge.

Branco: 'I wasn't really sure about preserve but I knew it had something to do with things that have been there a long time.'

Phillip and Le-Minh don't volunteer.

When the teacher had added these comments to her developing data bank of information about the five children involved in this retelling, she came to these tentative conclusions.

1. Chelsea and Leanne both feel confident and are in control. This control stems from background knowledge and experiences and the reception which they received from the other children. This confidence is reflected in their predictions and their willingness to make them public and elaborate on them in the sharing phase of the lesson.

2. Phillip and Le-Minh were both reluctant to share predictions which indicates a lack of confidence/control. Le-Minh has knowledge but is not yet confident enough to use it. Perhaps she hasn't yet come to grips with the concepts of prediction/speculation? Phillip lacks background knowledge.

3. Branco knows a lot about rainforests. He has obviously learned from the immersion and is confident to the degree that he is prepared to speculate. He is also confident enough to admit that he is guessing.

When the teacher checked some earlier evaluative opinions she'd made from observations of other retellings, she was able to put the two sets together and make the following inferences about Branco, Phillip and Le-Minh:

4. Branco, Phillip and Le-Minh were far more confident when speculating during fiction retellings. This suggests that they know that non-fiction has fewer degrees of freedom. There are more facts, which means more chances of being 'right' or 'wrong'. All three feel insecure with non-fiction and less in control than during retellings which involve fiction.

Everybody Read: Evaluation/Assessment Opportunity III

Another point in the retelling procedure sequence of events at which teachers can collect data for evaluative opinions is when participants are instructed to 'read the text as many times as you need to feel confident with the meaning'. One merely needs to observe how different readers go about this task. For example, here is a summary made from observational records of two of the children who took part in this particular retelling. They represent about 15 minutes of careful observation, with rough notes being made, as the observer swung her gaze from one student to the next, spending three to five minutes observing each one. The rough notes were later rewritten and reflected upon.

Phillip: • eye movement rapid and staccato
  • appears to be easily distracted from the reading task, and loses concentration and control at the slightest disturbance, e.g. a knock at the door
  • looks up from the text frequently, as if trying to sort something out.

Chelsea: • reads text from beginning to end without being distracted
  • when finished reading, looks back to earlier portions of texts, as if re-looking for some idea or point
  • appears to be very deeply engaged with the text

Evaluative opinion based on observations

Phillip is reading on a word-by-word basis. (This is unusual because in SSR he often loses himself in a book.) He appears to be trying to memorise rather than understand. The ease with which he is distracted by events around him suggests that Phillip is looking for an excuse to break with the text which he finds hard to process.

Chelsea reads as easily as if she were reading fiction. Her engagement is deep and full and she is not distracted by other events.

One prediction that could be made at this point is that Phillip's end product, i.e. his retelling text, will be 'off-beam'. However, one should remember that this in only a *rough* prediction based on a few evaluative opinions formed hastily. Predictions such as these must be held in check until all the evaluative opinions are collected.

Writing the Retelling: Evaluation/Assessment Opportunity IV

After the participants have read, they are expected to complete a written retelling of the text without referring to it again. Observations of how they do this will also provide data which can be used to form evaluative opinions. Here is a summary of observations made on the same two students (Chelsea and Phillip) while they were engaged in the task of rewriting their text from memory.

Chelsea: • When finished reading the text (and we suspect she read it only once), Chelsea stared into space for about 60 seconds
  • she turned text face down and picked up pen – and began writing and wrote for about two minutes
  • stopped writing and re-read what she had written
  • stared into space for about 30 seconds, started writing again

- repeated this cycle until finished task — took about 15 minutes all told
- proofread and added an exclamation mark

Phillip:
- appeared to read/re-read the text at least five times
- was slow to begin writing, and after being distracted by various insignificant events, stared out of window for a while
- when teachers announced 'We'll share in a few minutes', Phillip hastily wrote without stopping and re-reading
- made no attempt at proofreading

Evaluative opinions

Phillip has approached the task acting like a 'sponge', i.e. is trying to soak up what's on the page rather than understand it. His focus is on rote memory. There appear to be no rehearsal breaks during the writing of his text, nor any attempt at proofreading.

- Chelsea seems to want to produce a considerate retelling and appears to be using a well-known cycle of rehearse/write without interruption/read, rehearse/write/re-read, and so on, followed by proofreading.

Share and Compare: Evaluation/Assessment Opportunity V

After the written retelling, the next step is the sharing section, otherwise known as 'share and compare'. It begins typically with a statement from the teacher:

Teacher: 'It's time now to share and compare our retellings. When someone volunteers to share I want the rest of you to listen very carefully because I might call on you to react. Remember, all your statements must be justified, and they must be helpful and constructive.

The teacher then waits for volunteers to share their retellings. The exchanges which occur provide a wealth of data from which to form further evaluative opinions. Here is an example of the kind of exchanges which can occur during this phase of the lesson (taken from a video transcript).

Teacher: 'How did you find that piece of writing? Was it difficult or easy? Why?'

Chelsea: 'Easy, because we've been learning about rainforests and logging is really topical at the moment. Would you like to hear mine?' (See page 122).

Branco challenges Chelsea's detail.

Branco: 'That was a thorough retelling, Chelsea. But why didn't you say how long ago the destruction started?'

Chelsea: 'I did, I said ". . . at the time when Cook discovered Australia" and that means 200 years ago, because Cook discovered Australia in 1788.'

This exchange reveals the following:

1. The different levels at which Branco and Chelsea operate. Chelsea

9.7.86.   <u>Preserve our rainforest</u>

I think this writing is going to be about people
who want to keep the rainforests of Australia.

save conditions rainforest.

Many year ago(at the time when Captain Cook
discovered the east coast), their used to be
more rainforest. After Captain Cook people
cut down our rainforest for wood.
If no rainforests are left where will all the nature
of Australia be? Will anybody in the future see
one? No probaly not. Cus cus and tree kangaroo
only have rainforest as their home. Will they
survive? No probaly not. How would you like it
if you were about to have no home just beca
use someone needs wood? Would you like
it? Of course not so fight!

'SAVE OUR RAINFOREST'

has operated on the language at a level well beyond the literal level. She has established the same meaning ('200 years ago' through a second order of meaning ('at the time when Cook discovered Australia'). It suggests that she comprehended what she read at a very sophisticated level. Branco is obviously more comfortable at the literal level.

2. Both these children are confident to challenge and be answerable, and feel no apprehension about the 'give and take' of discourse and the clarification of meanings.

Later in the session, the video shows that Phillip and Le-Minh each made a contribution:

Phillip (restating the obvious): 'I liked your retelling, Chelsea, you've remembered to put everything in. It's similar to mine but you've used better words.'

9-7-86

> Presrve Our rain forest
> I think it is about people
> looking at rain forest.
>
> ---
>
> When Captan Cook came
> over all the convicks cut
> down all the red seader
> trees so their isn't much
> rain-forestc left the
> Guverment shod presrve
> all rainforests and make
> them into nashagtl rain-
> forests.

Le Minh: (always the diplomat): 'Chelsea's is like mine but she said it in a different way.'

These statements reveal the following:

1. Phillip's explanation of the difference between his and Chelsea's retellings is rather vague ('used better words'). He doesn't offer to justify why the words are 'better', or even which words they are.

2. Despite this, Phillip's actual text reveals that his comprehension of the material in the text wasn't as poor as the earlier evaluative opinions would have suggested. **This highlights the necessity of getting all the data in before drawing any firm conclusions.**

The Retelling Text: Evaluation/Assessment Opportunity VI

The actual texts which the participants in a retelling session produce are a rich source of data about the literacy knowledge they have under control. These 'products' can be analysed from many perspectives: which of these perspectives are the best ones to use?

The answer to this question is related to the aims and objectives the teacher has set and to the values that are held about what is important in literacy. Just as teachers' aims and objectives are ultimately based upon what they know and value about literacy and its various manifestations (reading, writing, spelling, speaking, and so on), so the kinds of things they'll analyse, weigh up and count in any retelling text, are based on similar knowledge and values. Therefore we cannot give a definitive set of analytical criteria which can be applied to retelling texts. Teachers must work these out for themselves.

Instead, we present some of the analytical criteria which we have found useful and explain how we have used them.

Evaluative opinions based on these data

When we looked closely at the retelling texts which the children in our experiment produced, and then tried to summarise and make explicit why we judged some to be indicative of more control over the written form of the language than others, we found that our values about what made a good retelling text centred on three broad areas of control: **meaning, structure** and **conventions**.

Under **meaning**, we asked two questions:
1. How clear and unambiguous are the main ideas (points, concepts, notions, etc)?
2. How appropriate to its purpose is the form or register of the text?

Under **structure**, we focused on a broad set of organisational aspects of text, such as the unity between the parts and the whole, the sequence of ideas, the quality of the leads, the nature of the paragraphs, the relationship between text and title.

Under **conventions**, we looked at the degree to which the child's piece showed control of spelling, punctuation and usage conventions.

The judgments we made were 'wholistic' ones and we recorded them in the form of short phrases. Here are the main evaluative opinions we made on the retelling texts produced by Chelsea, Phillip, Le-Minh and Branco, in response to the original text 'Preserve Our Rainforest'.

Chelsea (see page 122 for text):
Meaning
- argument identified, summarised, and clearly expressed
- main idea developed into her own argument
- good persuasive interpretation

Structure
- good lead
- appropriate paragraphing
- dramatic ending, appropriate to form and purpose
- text supports title

Conventions
- excellent control of spelling (99 conventionally spelled words to two unconventional or 99:2)
- appropriate vocabulary used
- correct syntax throughout
- control of question mark, comma, full stop, inverted commas and brackets

Phillip (see page 123 for retelling text):
Meaning
- argument identified, summarised and clearly expressed ·

Structure
- logically sequenced
- text supports title

Conventions
- good phonetic spelling approximation
- confusion with "isn't/aren't, much/many"

- used capitals with proper nouns appropriately
- text lacks punctuation

Le Minh (see page 133 for retelling text):

Meaning
- argument identified, summarised and clearly expressed
- good persuasive interpretation
- has used facts well

Structure
- uses good lead
- appropriately paragraphed
- logically sequenced
- text supports title

Conventions
- good attempts to spell words not in spoken vocab (142:14)
- errors in syntax commensurate with oral control of syntax
- correct punctuation
- use of hyphen

Branco

Meaning
• argument identified, summarised, clearly expressed
Structure
• good lead
• logically sequenced
• text supports title
Conventions
• good control of spelling (133:4)
• good use of hyphen
• improving control of simple punctuation

If you look back over the observations recorded in Evaluation/ assessment opportunities I–VI and summarise them for each child, you can make some interpretative statements about each child's ability to infer, predict, hypothesise and generalise. We have decided to call these 'cognitive abilities'. Here is an example of what we mean.

Cognitive abilities
Chelsea
• accurate prediction based on knowledge
• summarised and then assumed ownership of argument
• good use of rhetoric

Phillip
• couldn't make accurate prediction
• lack of background knowledge

Le-Minh
• tentative prediction but close to main idea
• literal recall

Branco
• understands the speculative nature of prediction
• confident in prediction though not accurate
• literal recall/retelling

If we combine all this store of information, it is possible to draw up a matrix which gives a very detailed picture of what levels of control each of these four children displayed during this particular retelling. A blank matrix is included in the Appendix for you to use if it suits your needs.)

'Preserve Our Rainforest'	MEANING	STRUCTURE	CONVENTIONS	COGNITIVE ABILITIES
	• ideas • clarity • relevance to form/ purpose of writing	• organisation of writing • unity between parts and whole • sequence	• spelling • usage • punctuation • appropriate vocab.	• ability to: —infer —predict —hypothesise —generalise
Chelsea	• argument identified, summarised and clearly expressed • main idea developed into her own argument • good persuasive interpretation.	• good lead/well paragraphed • dramatic and appropriate ending • text supports title	• excellent control of spelling (99:2) • vocab. appropriate, correct syntax • control of (?..!'' ''())	• accurate prediction based on knowledge • summarised and assumed total ownership of argument • good use of rhetoric
Phillip	• argument identified summarised and clearly expressed	• logically sequenced • text supports title	• good approximations phonetic (40:6) • 'isn't/aren't' 'much/many' confusions • used proper noun capitals; text not punctuated	• couldn't make accurate prediction • lack of background knowledge
Le-Minh	• argument identified summarised and clearly expressed • good persuasive interpretation—has used facts well	• good lead/well paragraphed • logically sequenced • text supports title	• good attempts at words not in her vocab (142:14) • syntactical errors in line with her speech • correct punctuation, use of hyphen	• tentative in prediction but close to main idea • literal recall/retelling
Branco	• argument identified, summarised and clearly expressed	• good lead • logically sequenced • text supports title	• good control of spelling (133:4) • correct use of hyphen • improving control of simple punctuation	• understands the speculative nature of prediction • confident in prediction though not accurate • literal recall/retelling

Using Retelling Data over Time

As well as mapping different children's performance on the same retelling, it is possible to map the same child's performances during different retellings over time. For example, let us compare how observations on Le-Minh's retelling behaviour looked over three retelling sessions between February and July.

The Goose and the Golden Eggs

There was once a poor farmer and his wife who bought a goose. The next morning when the wife went into the farmyard she found that the goose had laid a golden egg. The husband and wife were delighted at their good fortune. Every morning they found a golden egg under the goose and soon they grew very rich. They had everything that money could buy and wanted for nothing.

However, the richer they became, the greedier they became. One day the farmer's wife spoke to her husband saying: 'One golden egg a day is not enough. We need more. If we kill the goose we can get all the gold inside her at once.'

So together they killed the goose that laid the golden eggs, but they found no gold. The goose was just like any other goose. The husband got angry with his wife, saying: 'Your greed has ruined us. Why couldn't you have been satisfied with one golden egg a day?'

Moral: Be thankful for what you've got.

19.2.86   The Goose and the Golden eggs

I think the story of the Goose
and the golden eggs is about
a goose and a golden egg

There was once a poor
farmer and his wife bought
a goose. The next day when
his wife went out to get
some eggs, insect she found
a golden. From that day on
they grew richer and greeder.
One day his wife said, "One
golden egg a day is not any-
nofe so why don't we killed
the goose and get all the
gold out of it." So the next
morning they went into the
shed and killed the goose
but they found no gold in the
goose, be was angler with
his wife that he said, "you are
so greedy that you weren't

satisfild with one golden
egg a day and now we
have no more gold.

Death Alley

Neill Paxton (5th grade)

It was a cold harsh night and the wind was strong, blowing furiously through the never-ending alleys. It tossed up leaves and litter and turned them over with the least bit of care. This cycle took place time after time. Suddenly silence broke and there was a clash of garbage tins. A shadow covered the alley and a figure stumbled into sight. He huddled up into a corner of the alley. Slowly he raised the syringe into the air and gazed at it. With the most delicate touch the needle pierced the skin and drugs soon filled his body. As the street lights flickered he struggled to his feet. He followed the wall that was marked with graffiti. The night was long and the night was cold but the man fought for his life. Death was close and the rain pelted down on the garbage tins. The man crawled across the alley and paused for a while. The rain stopped and the man slowly stopped breathing.

4.4

Death Alley

I think this ~~stor stroy~~ story is about a person who was merder in a alley and from ~~that~~ day on they called it death alley.

~~It~~ was a cold harsh night the wind was blowing ~~and~~ fuiosly it lift up leaves and litter without a least of care, suddenly ~~stigh~~ sight boke a strange figure covered the alley ~~and~~ as man huddle himself up to a comer. ~~and~~ He hebd up a strange ~~obje~~ct.

it ~~os~~ a shrape needle priese his shin and drug filled his body. ~~As~~ the wind blew harder. The man eought for his life but slowly ~~his~~ ~~bre~~ he could hardly beath.

* through a never end- ing alley

Preserve Our Rainforest

Two hundred years ago Australia had large expanses of rainforest — lush areas of tall, densely packed trees — home to many unusual creatures.

However, the early settlers who followed Captain Cook, cleared and destroyed vast sections of this rainforest. They cleared land so that they could farm, run cattle and grow crops. They also destroyed much rainforest by logging the rich, red cedar trees which were wanted by furniture makers. Gradually our rainforest started to disappear — now there is not very much left.

Australia *must* realise that the rainforest which remains must be preserved; clearing for farming and logging for timber *must* stop now before all our rainforest is destroyed. Many animals need the rainforest to survive; the cuscus and tree kangaroo live only in rainforest. What will happen to them if we don't stop the destruction of our jungles? The government should preserve all rainforest as national parks so that all Australians, now and in the future, may enjoy their beauty.

9.7.86   Preserve our Rainforest

Th I think this pice of writing is going to be
about someone who going to tell you abot
a rainforest.
Rainforest, cutting, die, save.

2oo years ago Australia had expaness of
rainforest - lush of tall trees, dendly pack and
unvasall creature that live in the the rainforest.

Early settlers that came with Captain-
Cook destored and clear to the rainforest
of for land to farm, run cattle and
grow crops. Furiture makes needed
the red ceder trees to make F furiture. Soon they, nearly clear the whole
sectione of rainforest.

We Australian must reliese that the
number of rainforest left is all we
have, the goverment should preseved
the rainforest and make them into
native national park so the
Australian now and in the furture
will observed their beatie.

TEXT	MEANING	STRUCTURE	CONVENTIONS	COGNITIVE ABILITIES
Fable 'The Goose and the Golden Eggs' 19/2/86	• Comprehension and interpretation of fable obvious • Language appropriate to genre of fable but no moral explicitly stated	• Ideas sequenced correctly and story easy to follow	• Control of simple sentence format • Developing control of speech marks and contractions • Spelling 130:5 • Problem with inflexional endings	• Literal/logical prediction • Volunteered to share both prediction and retelling
Narrative 'Death Alley' 14/4/86	• Comprehension and interpretation sound • Meaning clearly expressed	• Valid attempt to capture the intensity of the original writing. This has probably influenced the less controlled flow of ideas (though her ideas are sequenced)	• Spelling 100:7 • Problem with inflexional endings (but in line with her speech)	• Good interpretation of title • Very keen to discuss the intensity of the original and her concern to capture it all and not use her own words which might lose 'the feeling'
Expository 'Preserve our Rainforest' 9/7/86	• argument identified, summarised and clearly expressed • good persuasive interpretation—has used facts well	• good lead/well paragraphed • logically sequenced • text supports title	• good attempts to spell words not in her vocab. (142:14) • syntactical errors in line with her speech	• tentative in prediction but close to main idea • literal recall/retelling

What the 'Store of Information' Collected Revealed
A Summary

Attitude
- Positive approach to retelling maintained over a wide variety of text types.
- More willing to volunteer/share with predictable texts particularly fiction.
- Always polite and sensitive towards other sharers.
- Often reads and writes on the same topic after retelling.

Processes
- Re-reads texts two to three times before retelling.
- Apparently re-reads/checks her writing as she retells.
- Has coped well with a wide range of text types.
- Finds it hard to proofread immediately after writing.
- Attempts to maintain vocabulary appropriate to the text she is retelling.
- Always produces a considerate retelling.
- Generally retellings are logically structured, ideas developed.

Control of Written Conventions
- Noticeable improvement in punctuation which is now coming automatically to her in retelling situation.
- Excellent approximations in spelling.
- Spelling developing well.

- Has a problem with inflexional endings particularly ed, ing, s—still in line with her speech.
- developing knowledge of the paragraph.

Observation in Other Language Situations—Le Minh
Le-Minh's language was observed in the following situations:
- Conferences
- Writing
- Reading
- Contract
- Sharing time
- Other curriculum areas

Attitude
- Very willing to 'have a go' in all writing activities, although not necessarily to share her results.
- Confidence is highest when sharing/working on fictional writing.
- Has produced several strong pieces of work of which she is (quietly) proud.
- In a sharing situation (whole class or small group) she is always well prepared, can substantiate her ideas.
- Borrows weekly without fail from library.
- Often takes class library books home.
- Likes to read in a corner without interruption.

Processes
- Has developed in her ability to construct a narrative.
- Writing shows her understanding of the power of adequate description.
- Seeks help of others only when she has struggled with a problem.
- Organises time and resources efficiently under contract.
- Sensitively edits her own work and counsels others accordingly.
- Has developed several strategies to overcome a 'block' when reading/writing.
- Can work independently.
- 'Spillover' effect from retelling (myth, atmosphere and non-fiction description).
- Categorises information before writing.
- Sound comprehension of all texts treated in whole-class situations.

Skills/Control
- Improved spelling noticeable, now includes words not in her spoken vocabulary.
- Final draft work exhibits full control of capitals, full stop, question mark, speech marks. With a little help, she can also use comma and exclamation mark.
- Syntax still a problem in all writing as are inflexional endings (but this is the same in her speech).

- Uses reference aids well (index, contents, map readings, dictionary, encyclopaedia).
- Uses headings/sub-headings appropriately in written work.

On combining these data with information collected on Le-Minh in other language/literacy events, her teacher was able to put together this descriptive account of Le-Minh's development over a seven-month period.

Le-Minh is developing into a competent language user. She is a resourceful person who can work independently for a sustained period of time. She takes responsibility for her own work — writing, editing, proofreading, and can justify argument when necessary.

Le-Minh, while diplomatic, is a developing 'risk-taker' especially in written encounters. She is becoming increasingly adventurous with vocabulary, usage and spelling. In oral situations she is more willing to participate in a small group situation, with information with which she feels more comfortable. At the present time this is mainly fictional material.

Le-Minh exhibits a good understanding of many of the elements of story in genre such as myths and fables, and in the value of descriptive writing. She has produced several strong pieces of writing which show this.

She also appears to see the value of sub-headings in some expository writing and used them well in relation to the organisation of information for a map of South America.

Being a NESB child, Le-Minh speaks two languages. At present, in English, she has problems with syntax and grammar. I feel that these will be overcome as she reads and interacts more.

Le-Minh's determination to learn and her positive attitudes have helped her to develop control of many of the conventions of writing. She now has control of simple sentencing, question and speech marks, to such an extent that they are evident in controlled writing tasks where she has minimal opportunity to proofread. Spelling has shown noticeable improvement and is an outcome of her commitment to reading and writing and her attitudes towards these tasks.

Le-Minh is also coming to terms with the skills necessary to process non-fiction and is already a competent user of reference materials. More exposure to expository text will help her to extend her understanding/control and consolidate her knowledge of such genre.

Conclusion

Retelling procedure, as we describe it in this book, was originally conceived as a possible 'seat-work' or a 'keep-'em-busy-and quiet' activity which would free teachers to engage in face-to-face direct teaching with small groups of children. It was only as we came to understand in more detail the nature of what has become known as the 'wholistic/natural approach to literacy learning', that we realised the full potential of this procedure as a language activity which brought together all the major modes of language use (listening, speaking, reading, writing) in ways that resembled the powerful learning processes involved in language acquisition. The more we explored different ways of manipulating the procedure, the more we found out about the ways in which young learners can be helped to internalise many of the processes, forms, and conventions of written language which they must come to control if they are to be empowered in our society. We think we've only just scratched the surface of the potential of this procedure as a language-learning activity. We're confident that teachers can take the few principles we've espoused in here and extend them through a multitude of variations, with a multiplicity of text forms.

Appendix

Black-line Masters

PROGRAM FORMAT

| TEXT TYPE: | Term: |
| | Weeks: |

PURPOSE

IMMERSION

RETELLING

RESPONSE

TEXT	MEANING
	• ideas
	• clarity
	• relevance to form/
	  purpose of writing
		STRUCTURE
		• organisation of writing
		• unity between parts
		  and whole
		• sequence
			CONVENTIONS
			• spelling
			• usage
			• punctuation
			• appropriate vocals
				COGNITIVE
				ABILITIES
				• ability to:
				  —predict
				  —infer
				  —hypothesise
				  —generalise

Bibliography

Aesop, *Aesop's Fables*, J. M. Dent & Sons, London, 1967

Anderson, H., *Fairy Tales*, Rand McNally, Chicago, 1916

Barkirtzidoy, A., 'The Lone Dog' from *Feather or Fur*, Basic Reader No. 9, Young Australia Reading Scheme, Thomas Nelson Australia, 1982

Brett, B., *The Travels of Marco Polo*, Collins, 1971

Cambourne, B. L., *Natural Learning and Literacy Education*, Ashton Scholastic, 1987(a)

——. 'The Nature of Whole-language', Plenary paper, 2nd South Pacific Reading Conference, Hobart 1987(b)

Cambourne, B. L. and Turbill, J. B., *Coping with Chaos*, Primary English Teachers' Association, Sydney, 1987(c)

Carroll, L., *Alice in Wonderland*, Bell and Hyman, London, 1985

Children's Britannica, Vols 5, 7, 13, 16, London, 1971

Christopher Columbus, Nelson, 1964

Chrome, F., *Rainforests*, Hodder and Stoughton, Sydney, 1982

Dahl, R., *Danny the Champion of the World*, Jonathon Cape, London, 1975

Durrell, L., *My Family and Other Animals*, Penguin, 1978

Explore Magazine, *The Loch Ness Monster*, Victorian Education Department (3), 1982

Fairley, A., *Rainforest*, Methuen Australia, 1981

Famous Explorers, Macdonald Junior Reference Library, 1972

Grimm's Fairy Tales, Abbey Classics, London, 1970

Haliday, M. A. K., Plenary Session 'Writing in Australia' Conference, Kuringai College, Sydney, August 1986

Harste, J. C., Burke, C. L. and Woodward, V. A., 'Children's Initial Encounters with Print', N.I.E. Grant proposal, 1979, 1980, sighted in Hardt, V. H. (ed.), *Teaching Reading with the Other Language Arts*, International Reading Association, Newark, Delaware, 1983, p.44

Hecke, H. R., *How Men Discovered the World*, Kaye and Ward Ltd, 1970

Hitching, F., *The World Atlas of Mysteries*, Pan Books, 1978

Ingram Judson, C., *Christopher Columbus*, Follett Publishing Co., 1960

James, Nuggett Jabangadi, 'Why the Kangaroo Hops' from *Djugurba, Tales from the Spirit Time*, ANU Press,

Kipling, R., *Just So Stories*, Macmillan, London, 1965

La Fontaine, Variety of his fables published by Oxford, Melbourne

Laycock, G., *Mysteries, Monsters & Untold Secrets*, Scholastic Book Services, 1978

Lewis, C. S., *The Lion, the Witch and the Wardrobe*, Puffin Books, Penguin, Middlesex, Harmondsworth, 1970

The Loch Ness Monster, Macdonald Mysteries, 1979

Norton, M., *The Borrowers*, J. M. Dent & Sons Ltd, London, 1975

Parker, S., *The Rainforest*, Bay Books Pty Ltd, Sydney, 1984

Pearce, P., *Tom's Midnight Garden*, Oxford, London, 1958

Sadyebath and Anson Lowitz, *The Cruise of Mr Christopher Columbus*, Scholastic Book Services, 1975

Sale, M., *A Teacher's Guide to Practical Science in the Primary School*

Sloane, P. and Latham, R., *The Prehistoric Giants*, Methuen Australia, 1986

Smith, F., *Writing and the Writer*, Holt, Rinehart and Winston, New York, 1981

Smith, D. and Newton, P., *In History Exploration*, Schofield & Sims Ltd, 1971

Stevenson, R. L., *Treasure Island*, Macmillan, N.Y., 1963

Thiele, C., *Storm Boy*, Rigby, 1986

Thompson, A., 'Death of a Cat' in *Junior Poetry Workshop*, Russell, N. and Chatfield, H. J., Nelson, 1982

Thurber, J., *The Thurber Carnival*, Penguin, 1956

Tolkien, J. R. R., *The Hobbit*, Allen and Unwin, London, 1979

——. *Lord of the Rings*, Allen and Unwin, London, 1969

White, E. B., *Charlotte's Web*, Hamish Hamilton, London, 1952

The Young Scientist Book of Spaceflight, Usborne Publishers, 1976

Acknowledgements

The book is written and finally published—let no one say it was easy. Authors may take credit if any is forthcoming, but many people contribute to the writing of a book and should be mentioned. In this case:

- Children—especially those in grade 5 at Balarang Public School, Oak Flats, in 1985/6, who willingly engaged in the retellings of a wide range of material, talked openly of their learning and inspired us with their knowledge and understanding of language.
- Ian Coogan, Max Green and Jan Turbill, educators, who were always supportive, enthusiastic and constructive in comment.
- Kerrie Tweddle of Wagga Wagga High school who, in 1982, first experimented with retelling procedure and helped identify the early bugs.
- Anne Duncan and Jenny Hogan who deciphered scribble and transformed it into legible type.
- Olwyn and Eric who persevered.

We thank you all.

Every effort has been made to clear permissions for world rights for the material in this textbook. However, in the event of an oversight, the publishers apologise and guarantee to make the due acknowledgement or amendment in a subsequent reprint.

Barkirtzidoy, Athina: 'The Lone Dog' from *Young Australia Basic Reader 9*. Reprinted by permission of Thomas Nelson Australia, Melbourne.

Dahl, Roald: Extract from *Danny: The Champion of the World*. Reprinted by permission of Jonathan Cape, London. Copyright © 1975 by Roald Dahl. For the US and Canada, reprinted by permission of Alfred A. Knopf Inc., New York.

Harste, Jerome C., Burke, Carolyn L. and Woodward, Virginia A.: Adaption from *Figure 5* from 'Children's Language and World: Initial

Encounters with Print' from *Reader Meets Author/Bridging the Gap*, editors: Judith A. Langer and M. Trika Smith-Burke. Reprinted by permission of International Reading Association, Newark, Delaware, USA.

Jabangadi James, Nugget: 'Why the Kangaroo Hops' from *Djugurba: Tales of the Spirit Time*. Reprinted by permission of the Australian National University Press.

Klein, Robin: Extract from 'Fang' from *Snakes and Ladders*. Reprinted by permission of J. M. Dent Pty Limited, Knoxfield, Victoria.

Maps of Australia and South America: From *Jacaranda Australian Primary Atlas*. Reprinted by permission of Jacaranda Cartographics, Milton, Queensland.

Pearce, Philippa: Extract from 'Aunt Gwen's House' from *Tom's Midnight Garden*. Reprinted by permission of Oxford University Press, Oxford, U.K.

Thurber, James: Extract from 'The Scotty Who Knew Too Much' from *Fables for Our Time/Vintage Thurber Vol 1*. Reprinted by permission of Hamish Hamilton Ltd, London. Copyright © 1940 James Thurber. Copyright © 1968 Helen Thurber. From *Fables For Our Time*, published by Harper & Row, Inc., New York. Reprinted by permission of Rosemary A. Thurber, Michigan, U.S.A.

White, E.B.: Extract from *Charlotte's Web*. Reprinted by permission of Hamish Hamilton Children's Books, London. Pages 13–14 from *Charlotte's Web* by E. B. White. Copyright 1952 by E.B. White. Text copyright renewed 1980 by E. B. White. Reprinted by permission of Harper and Row, Publishers, Inc., New York.